STONEY CREEK WOMAN

STONEY CREEK WOMAN

THE STORY OF MARY JOHN

Bridget Moran

ARSENAL PULP PRESS
Vancouver

STONEY CREEK WOMAN
Copyright © 1988 by Bridget Moran and Mary John
New preface © 1997 by Bridget Moran

THIRTEENTH PRINTING : 2004

ARSENAL PULP PRESS
103-1014 Homer Street
Vancouver, B.C.
Canada V6B 2W9
www.arsenalpulp.com

Originally published by Tillacum Library, a division of Arsenal Pulp Press.

The Publisher gratefully acknowledges the support of the Canada
Council for the Arts for its publishing program, and the support of
the Book Publishing Industry Development Program and the B.C.
Arts Council.

Typeset by the Vancouver Desktop Publishing Centre
Printed and bound in Canada by Printcrafters
Cover Photo: Mary John, 1965
Author Photo by Phyllis Parker

Photos reprinted with the permission of the Provincial Archives of
British Columbia, the *Prince George Citizen*, and Mary John.

CANADIAN CATALOGUING IN PUBLICATION DATA:
Moran, Bridget, 1923-
   Stoney Creek woman

   ISBN 1-55152-047-8

   1. John, Mary, 1913- 2. Stoney Creek Indian Reserve (B.C.)—
Biography. 3. Carrier Indians—Biography. 4. Indian women—
British Columbia—Biography. I. Title.
E99.T17J63 1997   971.'004972   C97-910480-7

This book is dedicated to my dearest daughter, Helen Jones, who inspired me to tell my story. Helen died on May 19, 1987, while the writing of this book was in progress.

—MARY JOHN

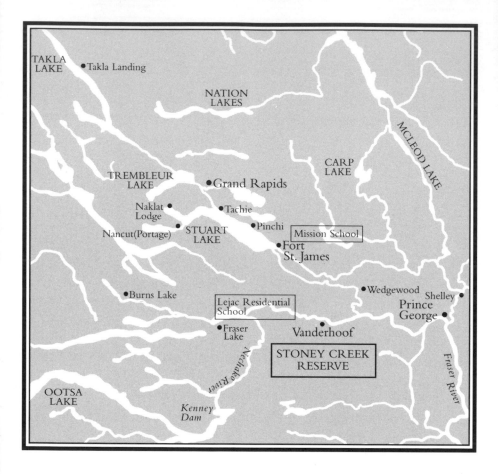

TAKLA LAKE
• Takla Landing

NATION LAKES

CARP LAKE

MCLEOD LAKE

TREMBLEUR LAKE

• Grand Rapids

Naklat Lodge •
• Tachie

Nancut(Portage) •
STUART LAKE
• Pinchi

Mission School

• Fort
St. James

• Burns Lake

Lejac Residential School

• Wedgewood
Shelley •
Prince George •

• Fraser Lake

Vanderhoof

STONEY CREEK RESERVE

Nechako River

Fraser River

OOTSA LAKE

Kenney Dam

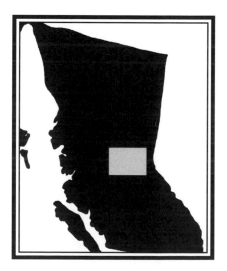

PREFACE TO NEW EDITION

ALMOST A DECADE HAS PASSED since Elder Mary John and I autographed the first copies of *Stoney Creek Woman*, a project which had begun with a simple letter ten years earlier. That initial book-signing on November 12, 1988 was the beginning of what Mary calls an adventure that has taken us both into undreamed-of places and relationships and events.

Although, as I write in the original introduction to *Stoney Creek Woman*, I feel as though I have known Mary John forever, in fact I first met her in 1976, when the people of Stoney Creek joined together to force the justice system to hold an inquest into the death of Coreen Thomas. The twenty-one-year-old Carrier Native was in her ninth month of pregnancy when she was struck and killed by a car driven by a young man named Richard Redekop. During the time before the inquest and for months afterwards, I was often in Mary John's home, and each time I came away warmed just by having been with her.

And the letter—it was written in 1977 by Mary's beloved

daughter Helen, and in it she asked me to write the story of her mother's life.

Regrettably, the letter has been lost, but I have not forgotten Helen's words. She wrote that she felt her mother's life was the story of many aboriginal women of Mary's generation. But more than this, wrote Helen, she believed that her mother had special qualities that should be set down in a book, so that future generations of First Nations could know her mother as her family and community knew her.

Regrettably, too, by the time Mary and I were in Mosquito Books in Prince George, B.C. that cold November day in 1988, Helen had passed away. Nevertheless, before she died, she knew the book was underway. For months, even years after her letter to me, on weekends and during summer holidays, she would discover my little motorhome parked beside her mother's house. She could have predicted the scene she would find inside: her mother glancing out over Nulki Lake, her hands endlessly busy with her beadwork, and me, across from her, knitting at a fairly frantic pace—I was trying, successfully I might add, to quit smoking. A cheap little taperecorder was between us on Mary's big work table, quietly spinning away, recording for all time our words, our laughter, our anger, and sometimes our tears.

In the years since the publication of *Stoney Creek Woman*, Mary John and I have criss-crossed British Columbia many times. In villages and cities, on reservations in the Nass Valley and off the coast of Prince Rupert, in the heart of Vancouver Island and on reserves closer to home in the central part of the province, we have visited schools, colleges and universities, and attended head-start programs, conferences, workshops and meetings of every kind. We have also become more deeply involved in each other's lives: Mary has invited me to potlatches, wakes, funerals, and gatherings on her reserve. She comes to my parties, my special events, and I have taken to calling my spare room "Mary's room." Unless one or the other of us is travelling, we talk on a weekly basis, sometimes more.

During our travels together, an interesting transformation has taken place in the way we refer to *Stoney Creek Woman*. We began by describing it as "my book about Elder Mary John." Imperceptibly the description changed to "our book," and then, without either one of us quite knowing how or when the change occurred, it became, and remains, "Mary's book."

Again, imperceptibly, over the years we developed a routine in our public appearances—I make the speeches and, for the most part, Mary answers the questions. We talk about everything: the residential school system, life on Stoney Creek, racism, the potlatch system, the Elders Society, the Catholic Church, her work to preserve the Carrier language and culture, her health, her concerns about poverty and unemployment, her arranged marriage, and how *Stoney Creek Woman* was written, including her refusal to let me put any word about sex into the book. There are no areas of her life, nor in mine for that matter, which are off limits when we appear together.

And during these public functions, there is much laughter.

There is the story Mary tells of the young person learning the Carrier language who believed she was asking for the time when in fact she was saying, "White man's ear." There is also the tale of the youths who wanted to make traditional food and deliver it to the Stoney Creek elders in their homes. "They told me they wanted to make fish head soup," Mary says, "and asked me what to do. I told him to get fish heads, water, a little salt, some onion and potato, and to let them boil. The young people told me they decided to try the soup themselves, but when they saw the fish head in the dish, they said, 'Yuk! It's looking at us!' and they couldn't eat it. So they put the soup in the elders' van to deliver it, but it spilled. The van smells like fish to this day!"

Needless to say, each of us has a life that is active and apart from the other. Mary John is involved in clan gatherings, justice committees, land claim hearings, Carrier assemblies, child welfare committees, economic development planning sesssions, and institutes dedicated to preserving Carrier language and culture. And with it all, she is a loving mother, grandmother, great-grandmother, and great-great-grandmother; at last count she had thirty grandchildren, thirty-one great-grandchildren, and three great-great-grandchildren.

She has received many honours. In 1992 she was awarded the Governor General's Medal commemorating the 125th anniversary of the Confederation of Canada. In 1996 the University of Northern British Columbia bestowed an Honorary Doctor of Laws degree on her, in recognition of her many years of service to her people. At an Elders Society dinner to celebrate this award—the elders called it her graduation dinner—the Carrier Sekani tribal chief, Linda Prince, presented her with a cape; a caribou, symbol of Mary's clan, was outlined on the back. And in April 1997 she travelled to Ottawa to receive the Order of Canada from the Governor General.

———————

A question that Mary John is often asked is, "Since your story has been published, what has been good, and what has not been so good, about your life?"

Mary replies that in 1976, when her people organized to demand an inquest into Coreen Thomas' death, Stoney Creek reserve was one of the poorest reservations in British Columbia—its statistics for unemployment, inadequate housing and living conditions, violence and alcohol abuse were among the highest in the province. "Now," says Mary, "that is changed. Our population is growing, we have new housing, we have sewer and water service which we didn't have in 1976, the road through our reserve is paved, our Elders Society is strong and active, and above all we have many of our young people employed. We have about a dozen men working in the bush for Neduchen (Our Wood) managing a tree license, and seventy-five men and women are employed in Dezti Wood—a joint venture involving three reserves to process value-added wood. It took us twenty years of struggle with the Department of Indian Affairs to get these opportunities for our young people, but at least we have them now."

On a more somber note Mary adds that the town of Vanderhoof, where Stoney Creek residents spend hundreds of thousands of dollars each month, does not employ Natives—her people find work only within their own community. Racism and unemployment, she says, are still facts of life for many young people on her reserve.

But it is when Mary speaks of what has not been good in her personal life that grief drops her voice almost to a whisper. She tells her listeners that she has lost two beloved daughters, Helen and Winnie, since her book was begun. And on Good Friday, 1996, she lost her husband Lazare. If he had lived until June of that year, they would have celebrated sixty-seven years of married life.

I was at Lazare's wake in the loghouse they built together, overlooking Nulki Lake, and along with an overflow crowd, I attended his funeral in Stoney Creek village. My eyes blurred as I watched Lazare's last trip down the slight incline to the Catholic Church, where he had been church chief for so many, many years. His son Ernie and granddaughter Sarah led the procession on horseback. They were followed by Lazare's old friend Walt Dettwiler driving a team of horses hitched to an ancient wagon. Inside the wagon was Lazare's body in the plain pine box he had requested his friend, Elder Nick Prince of Fort St. James, to make to serve as his coffin. He was dressed in his church clothes—Lazare had never worn a suit—and his familiar tweed cap was resting on his chest.

With her grandson Fabian, with nephews and grandchildren and great-grandchildren dropping in for meal or a place to stay, Mary shares her home. As she approaches her eighty-fourth birthday, her pace has, if anything, quickened. By car and bus and plane, sometimes by boat, she goes from one end of the province to the other, still pursuing her Carrier dream.

She spoke of her dream at the end of her book when it was first published in 1988.

"We must keep our language, our culture," she said then, "so that, even in Canada, we can still feel that we have our own country. And while we preserve these things, it is my hope that some day we will also have reserves where the young can be educated, where there is employment for all and where my people will choose to live, and work, and finally, to die and rest in peace."

That dream has not changed.

—BRIDGET MORAN
Prince George, B.C.
Spring 1997

INTRODUCTION

LIKE A LONG DISTANCE ROMANCE, my intimacy with Stoney Creek Indian Reservation has been sporadic but persistent.

I made the first of many trips to the reserve in 1954. As a social worker for the provincial government, I soon found myself caught up in a labyrinth of jurisdictions. This business of jurisdictions dates back to the year 1871, when British Columbia joined Canada. In that year, the federal government assumed complete control of all reservations in the province.

By the time I was employed by the provincial government, there was one exception to this total control—if a complaint was received that a reserve child was neglected or abused, a provincial social worker or a worker with a Children's Aid Society was required to conduct an investigation. If evidence of either neglect or abuse was discovered, the child was removed to a foster home, which, in practise at least, always turned out to be a white home. This mandate to give protection to a child, through removal from a reserve, was the sum total of our service to reserve life; intervention to prevent abuse or neglect while the child remained in his own home on the reserve was not part of the job. All the tools of prevention—food, clothing, health services—were controlled by the Indian Agent, an employee of the federal government, and were dispensed by him.

In the 1950s and early '60s, my colleagues and I dreaded these mandatory forays to reserves. In villages like Stoney Creek, we came face to face with poverty such as we had never seen before. Sad to say, when the Natives pleaded for food or clothing, we were helpless. We could do nothing except explain jurisdictions. "We can't help you!" we would say. "We work for the provincial government and it is the federal government who looks after you. You should see your Indian Agent and get him to help you."

The most wretched trip that I made to Stoney Creek Reserve was in 1955. My mother, Rose Anne Drugan, who throughout her own life had had much first-hand experience with poverty, accompanied me. I have no memory as to why I was on the reserve that day—probably it was another complaint of child neglect. What I do remember is that within minutes, when the residents of Stoney Creek recognized the car as a government vehicle, they surrounded me, crying for help. Almost all the pleaders were women.

"My husband is in Millar Bay Hospital with T.B. and I have no food."

"Please, my husband can't find work. Help me!"

"My children have no shoes and winter is coming! Please help me!"

"Help me!"

"Help me!"

Mary John and I have since wondered if she was in that group of desperate women. Perhaps she was. Many of them had rags wrapped around their feet; their clothes were pitiful to see and their faces were lined and haggard.

I was ashamed then, and I am ashamed to this day, that I

could do nothing for them. When I returned to the car, tears were coursing down my aged parent's face.

"Bridgie," she said, "you will have to do something to help these people!"

"I will, Mother of Mine," I promised. "I will." This book is part payment of the promise I made to my mother that afternoon.

Meanwhile that day in the fall of 1955, I drove the nine miles back to Vanderhoof. As I had done so many times before, I tracked the Indian Agent to his lair and demanded that help be given to the women of Stoney Creek. As I recall, I was given a half-hour talk on the theme, "You can't do anything with an Indian!," followed finally by a grudging promise to visit the reserve himself.

Another memory of a time, thirty years ago or more. . . .

I had been in court in Vanderhoof during the morning, giving evidence of the abuse of a reserve child we will call Theresa. The local doctor, long since gone from Vanderhoof, had made the initial complaint and that morning gave a scaring description of his examination of the child—her body, he said, was covered with bruises and lacerations. Finally, after a distressing three hours of sworn evidence, court was adjourned for lunch.

As a matter of course, I asked the Natives present, including Theresa's parents, to join me for soup and a sandwich. We walked together to the local café. When we got to the door, the Natives moved back.

"Come on," I said impatiently. "I'm dying for a cup of coffee!"

They shook their heads. "We can't go in there."

And then of course I remembered—this restaurant did not serve Natives.

I started to suggest that we go in, Irish and Indian together, and make a kind of Custer's Last Stand against this racism. Midway through my plea, I stoppped; the looks of horror on

their faces told me a million stories of discimination, humili-
ation, fear.

Back in court that afternoon, I thought that there had to be
some terrible connection between this charge of child abuse
and the refusal of a second-rate café to serve Indians. In court,
we heard of one Native's anger allegedly turned inward
against his own child. I wondered if in the years to come that
anger would ever move outward against the white community. One day, I thought, it will surely happen.

Considering my many trips to Stoney Creek over the years,
I was certain that I had met Mary John sometime back in the
1950s. "Not so!" she says—that we met only in 1976, at the
time of the inquest into Coreen Thomas' death. I have always
found this hard to believe; Mary, with her quiet voice, her
ready laugh, the care with which she translates feelings into
words, seems to have been a part of my life for as long as I
have driven the roads of central British Columbia.

Whatever date is the correct one, I have vivid memories of
Mary at that inquest. I remember watching her gather some of
the young people together, speaking softly to them, advising
them to tell the truth when they answered questions before
the coroner and the jury. I remember her sitting with her
daughter Helen, listening to each word spoken at the inquest,
that classic face of hers reflecting anger, horror, amusement.
And I remember her at her kitchen table during one of the
nights of the inquest, when she and her family played host to
reporters and lawyers and fellow travellers like myself. I
watched her as she mingled with this mixed bag of people; it
was only afterwards, as we talked in the gathering twilight
one evening, that I realized how unusual this levee at her
kitchen table had been, and that there had been both strain
and excitement that night for her.

After the inquest, I saw Mary John in many different settings. As the years passed and our relationship deepened, I
discovered that her character has neither the simplicity nor

the passivity which people who have never known an Indian nor set foot on a reservation like to attribute to 'The Noble Savage.' She retains her youthful shyness, but with this she displays the courage becoming to an elder of an Indian band.

Time after time, as we talked together, I have heard her reconcile the irreconcilables, and laugh at the doing of it. I attended the Roman Catholic Church in Stoney Creek village with her, for example, and I heard that wonderful voice of hers soar over all other parishoners as she sang, "How Great Thou Art." Back in her house after Mass, she told me the story of how, years before, a priest had tried to excommunicate her husband, herself, and her children. She described how she and her family had ignored the priest and attended Mass as if he had never spoken the terrible word 'excommunication.' She laughed as she told me of this defiance. She is a devout Roman Catholic who can talk about the hard-heartedness of nuns and priests when she attended residential school; nevertheless, one of her closest friends is an Irish nun. She attends church regularly but will say without hesitation, "The government and the church almost destroyed our language, our culture!"

I have seen Mary in so many settings: starting out with a member or two of her family when the fish are running, and learning afterwards that she had handled the canoe and organized the nets herself; seeing her at a potlatch with other elders, counting money for payouts with as much dexterity as a teller in the Royal Bank; keeping a death watch over her daughter Helen in the Intensive Care Ward of the Prince George Hospital; conducting a guided tour of the Potlatch House and grounds, pride and hope for the future giving a ring to her voice.

But most often when I think of Mary, I see an outdoor kitchen across from her log house. I always make certain that I visit Stoney Creek when the fish are running—late July and early August are my favourite times, for then we live outside for many hours of each day and the outbuilding becomes the centre of family life. Each year this workplace has been improved so that now, with its tin roof, its boards halfway up the sides, and its floor scattered with sawdust, protection is provided from winds or a sudden summer shower. There are work tables and cupboards and an old cook stove. An open fire of brick and grates used to be inside the structure; it smoked too much and is now outside, but still close enough for people to sit around. The cook stove and the homemade fireplace have fires burning, and on their tops are large pans. Water bubbles away in these pans, preserving the fish stuffed into sealers which Mary and her daughters have put in the pans hours before.

When the run of fish is good, fifty of more salmon are prepared for winter food each day. Some of the fish are cut into fillets and hung in the smokehouse, some are wrapped in heavy brown paper and placed in the deep freezer. What's left is in sealers, the boiling water around them filling the air with a gentle thrumming. In this outdoor room, Mary's children and grandchildren come and go endlessly, and cars and trucks move up the driveway at all hours. Mary's husband Lazare, now in his eighties, takes his meal of fried salmon and potatoes at one of the tables and then goes back to raking the yard or spray-painting his pickup truck. His endless activity forms a background for the work at tubs and benches and fires in the outdoor kitchen.

And as the darkness of night approaches, in the peace after activity, I have my favourite times with Mary. Often, her voice soft, she will talk of the past, perhaps about her young mother whom she lost years ago, or about how marriages were arranged when she was a girl. She orders me to put nothing about her own marriage into the book I am writing about her. "What," I say, "is there to be no sex at all in this book?" "No sex!" she says firmly, and we laugh together. Mary's laughter is close to the surface and, like her speech, it is always gentle.

But when Mary talks about her people's past, there is no laughter in her voice. She knows as do all the elders in Stoney Creek that there was a time, not many decades ago, when anthropologists and sociologists and the Natives themselves questioned whether her people, the Carrier, would survive.

In 1932, Diamond Jenness, a noted anthropologist and ethnologist, published a comprehensive work entitled *The Indians of Canada*. Writing about Mary John's tribe, the Carrier, he had this to say about the chances of Carrier survival: ". . . the Carrier do not understand the complex civilization that has broken like a cataract over their heads, and they can neither ride the current nor escape it. The white settlers around them treat them with contempt and begrudge them even the narrow lands the government has set aside for them. So they will share the fate of all, or nearly all, the tribes of British Columbia and disappear unnoticed within three or four generations."

Jenness could be forgiven for believing that the Carrier would disappear as a distinct group before the end of the present century. He was writing at a time when the Carrier were just beginning their slow climb back from a fate that had seemed to be inevitable—total extinction.

These Carrier who were Mary's forebears and who seemed at one time doomed to total extinction—where did they come from? Was it east over the Rockies, as some anthropologists have claimed, or did they come from the north, crossing the Bering Strait from Asia into North America? The authorities also disagree in their number. Were there 8,500 or 12,000 Carrier living in the central part of British Columbia, between the Rockies and the Coastal Range, before the advent of the white man? No matter which figure is the correct one, by 1890, after years of struggle with smallpox, measles, and venereal diseases, and with their food supply depleted, their total number was at an all-time low of 1,538 people. In the year that Mary John married, 1929, the number of Carrier had climbed only to 2,145, and in her own band in Stoney Creek, the number was a mere 166.

Until recently, because the struggle for survival was such a desperate one, the Carrier had neither the knowlege nor the energy to look beyond the Rockies and discover the kind of musical chairs game the mandarins in Ottawa were playing with their livelihood. The agency which made life and death decisions for them, Indian Affairs, was shuffled from one federal department to another over the years: from Secretary of State to the Department of the Interior, to the Department of Mines and Resources and, in 1950, in the strangest union of all, to the Department of Citizenship and Immigration. Its latest incarnation is the Department of Indian and Northern Affairs.

Along with D.I.A., the Indians are governed and bedevilled by a legal entity called the Indian Act. This Act, passed in 1876, delved into every facet of Native life—education, health services, welfare, taxes, rights concerning fishing and hunting, the consumption of alcohol, the right to vote, even the right to loiter in a poolroom!

Periodically, through pressure from Natives, the Indian Act has been revised. This was especially true after the Second World War. An Indian who joined the armed forces and who had been accepted as a first class citizen away from his own country, was no longer content to accept the fact that once back in Canada, he could not enter a polling booth, a pub, or a liquor store, and that he was still required to go, hat in hand, to the Indian Agent when he wanted to make even the smallest change to his life on the reserve.

One of the first restrictions to be lifted in the post-war period was the ban on potlatching. This social custom, so important to Natives for establishing social status, sharing goods, and repaying services, was forbidden in a section of the Indian Act in the nineteenth century. As a result, many bands held secret potlatches. This prohibition was finally lifted in a 1951 revision of the Indian Act, allowing potlatching to flourish once again.

The original Indian Act also prohibited Natives from drinking alcohol or having it on a reservation. In 1951 a revision of the Act allowed them to drink in pubs and bars. A further amendment in 1956 led to alcohol being allowed on the reserves and therefore, by definition, in the homes of Indians living on reserves. Similarly, the first version of the Indian Act denied Natives the right to vote, either provincially or federally. A revision of the Act in 1960 allowed them to vote in federal elections. (British Columbia had enfranchised Indians eleven years earlier.)

So the Act could be changed—but in the eyes of Mary John and her people, with such leaden feet did the bureaucrats in Ottawa move to redress the excesses of the Act!

Even more frustrating than the slow evolution of the Indian Act is the fact that this Act is administered by a federal government official, the Indian Agent.

Almost always a white man, the Indian Agent for the Carrier Bands was based in Vanderhoof until 1964; since that time, the Indian Affairs office has been located in Prince George. To Mary as a child and as a young woman, the Indian Agent was an all-powerful being, and indeed as a social worker, I found him scarcely less intimidating. In the years during which I worked for the provincial government, the Indian Agent and his officers had almost total control over the health, welfare and education of the aboriginal people. He gave out food rations, and on occasion, clothing and blankets; he authorized medicines and exercised control over health facilities for Natives; he worked with missionaries and religious organizations to establish schools, away from reserves if possible. Essentially, the Indian Agent and his staff *were* the Indian Act—the only check on them was a bureaucrat across the mountains in Ottawa, which was often no check at all.

My friends in Stoney Creek tell me that the Indian Agent of today and his officials are less remote than they were thirty or forty years ago. The racism practised so openly by Indian Agencies when Mary was a young woman would not be tolerated today—the Charter of Rights and "Red Power" have seen to that! This does not mean that the Indian Agency is a mere rubber stamp, passively approving everything the Natives demand. On the contrary, the power of the Indian Agency and of the Indian Act itself is as real as ever. The Natives to whom I talk confirm what Michael Kew wrote in 1986: that the still-existing sections of the Act "restrict Indians' ability to use reserve land, to spend money in the band's name, to enact by-laws and plan community business—in short, to undertake anything of importance or significance for themselves. In all such actions, hovering more or less imminently in the background, is the personage of the Indian Agent and his staff, who may veto, and must approve and process almost anything that a band council wishes to do on behalf of its membership."

Small wonder Mary John and her people often reflect that the more things change, the more they stay the same!

———————

Into the evolving hodge-podge of scattered reserves, with missionaries and Indian Agents trying to move her people towards acceptance of the white ways, and with her parents and elders striving to maintain the old traditions, my friend Mary John was born.

She was born at a time when her people struggled merely to survive in a white world. She has watched them multiply—her own band had grown from 166 in 1929 to over 540 today, with 375 living in Stoney Creek itself. She has lived to see her people feel pride in the Carrier name.

In her village live Celena and Veronica and Sophie and Agatha and many many more women whose life stories run parallel with hers. That is why it is important that the story of Mary John should be set down.

—BRIDGET MORAN
Prince George, B.C.
Summer 1988

PROLOGUE

"LONG AGO THERE WAS NO VILLAGE here at Stoney Creek. Tatchik, down about a mile, Nulki, at the end of Nulki Lake, and Laketown, four miles up the lake—these were the only places people lived. They lived in these places because of the fish. This was before 1890. All there was, was a trail going through where Stoney Creek is now.

"One man made a residing place just below where the graveyard is now and from then on, people started moving into the village of Stoney Creek, one at a time.

"They all started moving in from Tatchik and Nulki Lake on account of the fish spawning up Stoney Creek. People were dependent for their livelihood on fish and that is why, you see, every Indian village is by a lake or a river wherever there is fish.

"At Stoney Creek, year after year, as the season comes and goes, the people were preparing the food, like berries in the summer and the fish, and the hunting went on.

"Years and years ago, even before my time, the children

were educated to make a living. The boys went everywhere with their fathers and when the girl is old enough, her too, the mother takes over and starts training that child. How are they going to preserve the food, because food was very important, so it doesn't get spoiled—that is what the boys and girls are learning.

"So the girls are learning to preserve the food and prepare the food for drying, and the boys are in the bushes learning how to preserve and to skin—that is what the boys are doing. And when these young people are old enough and are married, they just know exactly what to do, so they don't depend on parents anymore.

"That is how it was, from generation to generation."

—ADNAS ALEXIS, *age eighty-*
five, speaking many years
ago in the Carrier language

CHAPTER ONE

MY VERY FIRST MEMORY is of the 1918 flu and of my young mother being very sick.

I was five years old. Like the other families on Stoney Creek Indian Reserve, we were living in a log cabin. I remember that people came in and out of our home, and that all of them talked about the 1918 flu that was sickening many Natives on the reserve, but what nineteen-eighteen meant or what kind of a terrible thing a flu might be, I did not know.

I remember that my eighteen-year-old mother, usually so busy with hides and fish, was very sick. To see her lying quietly on the homemade bed in the corner scared me.

One of the people who came to our home was the priest, Father Coccola. He talked to the mother of Agnes George, who was nursing my mother, and told her to make chicken soup.

My mother wouldn't touch the chicken soup. All she wanted was a cup of warm water. As if she was speaking now, I can hear her say, "Mary, put a cup of water on the stove. I am very thirsty."

That cup of water on the back of the stove and my mother asking for it—that is my first memory.

When a child is five years old, there is much that is confused and beyond understanding.

There was more than the 1918 flu which I did not understand. I didn't know why I had been called Mary Quaw for what seemed to me a long time, and then—I felt that it happened all of a sudden—I became Mary Paul, and I had a father called Johnny Paul and a sister called Bella.

I was much older before I could sort out all the happenings which brought me, a five-year-old, to a log cabin on Stoney Creek Indian Reserve, with sick people all around me.

———————

I suppose the real beginning was my great-grandmother, Mary Quaw, a widow. This was not the name by which most people knew her. She was called Six-Mile Mary because, although she belonged to the Fort George Indian Band, she had a cabin at Six-Mile Lake. This was some miles east of Fort George, the reservation just at the spot where the Nechako and Fraser Rivers meet in Central British Columbia.

I do not know why my great-grandmother set up her camp on the edge of Six-Mile Lake. No one knows what year she decided to build a cabin there, but I know that by the time I was born white men were filing claims for the land all around her. Maybe she found the village of Fort George too crowded for her liking. It might be that she spent many years of her life on the edge of Six-Mile Lake because there she found it easier to provide for her family with fishing and trapping and hunting.

When I was a little girl, I remember hearing the elders talking about Six Mile Mary. They used to say that she was 'hard.' To the elders, this meant not hard-hearted, but tough. She must have been hard, in their sense, and strong too. She brought up her sons and daughters through her own efforts.

There was no welfare, no assistance from the Department of Indian Affairs—she raised her family by herself. She had a few cows, a boat, a gun, and a cabin, and with these things she fed and clothed her large family.

This Six-Mile Mary, my great-grandmother . . . who was she? What was her maiden name? What was the name of her husband, my great-grandfather? When was she born? When was she married?

I don't know. It is only a guess that she was born around 1850 or even a few years before. The few pictures of her were taken when she was quite an old lady. People like my great-grandparents, my grandparents, even my mother, couldn't read or write. They weren't born in hospitals, they didn't register births or have land or houses in their own names. They didn't go through immigration to come into Canada. They never dreamed of owning such a thing as a camera—roots are very hard to trace when only the spoken word records a family's history.

How often I've wished that I had listened to the stories of the elders when I was a little girl! How often I've regretted the questions I never thought to ask my mother or my grandmother! The elders I could have listened to, the mother and grandmother I could have questioned, all, all are gone, and with them have gone, almost as if they had never existed, most of the records of Six-Mile Mary and her husband, their parents, their children.

But still there are the pictures. One shows Six-Mile Mary and my mother, who was then about fourteen, with a white man. They are standing at her camp on the edge of the lake. Six-Mile Mary was well past middle age when this picture was taken. There she is with her bandana knotted over each ear, her white hair falling to her shoulders, her face weather-beaten, cheerful, her hands and her body those of a woman who has spent most of her life out-of-doors. In this same picture my mother stands rigidly, arms pressed into her body.

On her face is a smile which looks ready to break into laughter. In another picture Six-Mile Mary is striding along the
road, away from the lake, and following close behind her is
my mother. As in the other picture, my mother is in a long
dress, her shoulders covered in a shawl, and her hair, like the
old woman's, is tucked into a bandana.

I do know that one of Six-Mile Mary's sons married my
grandmother Ann. This son and Ann had one child, a daughter, Anzell, who was my mother, that same girl following
Six-Mile Mary in the picture taken so long ago.

My Grandmother Ann told me what happened when my
mother Anzell was two years old. The men were out on the
trapline in McGregor, east of where Prince George is now.
My grandfather was with them. Suddenly he took sick and
died. No one ever told me what caused his death. My Grandmother Ann said that Six-Mile Mary's family came back to
Fort George to get more people so that her husband's body
could be brought back to the village. This must have happened about the year 1902.

Many many years ago, long before the time of Six-Mile
Mary and Ann and Anzell, a widow in our tribe carried the
ashes of her dead husband on her back for a very long time.
This is how we came to be called Carriers.

Even in my grandmother's time, life could be hard for
widows. Ann did not have to carry her husband's ashes
around with her, but something much harder happened to
her. Six-Mile Mary sent her back to her own people in Fort
George, and the old woman kept Ann's child. She raised
Anzell as her own and it was as if Ann had never had a
daughter.

Six-Mile Mary brought up my mother Anzell as she had
raised her own children in the cabin on the edge of the lake.
Anzell did not go to school—the only school for Natives at
that time was 150 miles away near Williams Lake—but the
little girl was Six-Mile Mary's companion, and she learned

early to hunt and fish, to treat hides, to trap, and to smoke and dry food for the winter.

My mother was the quietest person I have ever known. The elders said that she was like that even as a little girl. She used to go about her chores silently, always in Six-Mile Mary's shadow. These elders said the old woman was good to Anzell. "She'd do anything for that child!" they said.

White men used to come out to my great-grandmother's camp and rent her dugout canoe for trout fishing. I've heard stories that her regular charge for the use of her boat was fifty cents and a fifteen cent packet of tobacco for her old pipe. They used to try to buy her off with seventy-five cents, but no—fifty cents and a packet of tobacco was the going rate and she would not settle for a different arrangement!

One of these white men was a man called Charlie Pinker, an Englishman. He and his brother Ernie had come into the Fort George area and had taken up land between the reserve at Fort George and Six-Mile Lake. Charlie Pinker got my mother in the family way with me when she was only thirteen years old.

My mother never mentioned Charlie Pinker's name to me. Whether this man was often at Six-Mile Lake and waited for an opportunity to find Anzell alone, or whether he was there only once and raped her, I do not know. When I was already a grown woman, my Grandmother Ann spoke of Anzell's pregnancy to me. She said, "Your mother was just a child. She was so innocent, always with her grandmother. She knew nothing about men, nothing!"

Whatever happened between Anzell and Charlie Pinker, there was my mother—thirteen years old, with a baby girl. Six-Mile Mary was an old woman who was too frail and tired to start raising another child. The only good thing which came out of it all was that my Grandmother Ann had her daughter back with her, along with a baby. From then until my mother married Johnny Paul in 1917—I was four years old in that year and my mother was seventeen—we lived with my Grandmother Ann, and it was in those first four years that I was called Mary Quaw.

To this day, I feel a grudge against Charlie Pinker. He died a rich old bachelor, but he never gave a single penny to my grandmother or my mother or me. Times were often so hard that a helping hand from this man who was my father, and who knew that he was my father, would have made all the difference. If he had any feeling of responsibility about seducing an innocent girl of thirteen, he never showed it—there was not a dollar bill from him, not a pair of shoes or a coat, nothing!

Old ladies on the reserve who knew my history used to say to me, when Charlie Pinker was still alive, "You're going to be a rich woman when he dies!" Well, he must have taken his money with him—none of it ever came to me!

I never saw Charlie Pinker until after I was a married woman, although his brother Percy was good to me and we met often. Then one day I went to my father's house with some of Percy's family. What a strange meeting! Charlie Pinker talked to me as he would have talked to any young woman who visited in his home for the first time.

I've thought about that meeting often and when I remember it, one impression stays with me—a stranger sitting in that room with us would never have guessed that he was my father!

CHAPTER TWO

I MAY NOT HAVE KNOWN what the 1918 flu was, but I knew that it made me very sick. Sick as I was, I was aware that many things, some good and some very sad, were happening on the reserve.

Agnes George's mother stayed in our cabin until my mother was over the worst of her sickness. My mother was expecting a baby, and one day, when I was still in bed, this elderly woman came to me and told me that I had a new baby brother and that his name was Mark. Soon after she said this, Agnes George's mother said, "Well, I'd better get back to my own home. Everyone is sick there too."

A few days later, we heard that she was dead. Oh, the number of people who died on the reserve in those months was awful.

Our mission bell rings when someone dies. It seemed to me that, day and night, as the flu sickened more and more people, the bell never stopped ringing. I remember wishing that the ringing and the sickness and the deaths would end.

There was a doctor in Vanderhoof, Doctor Stone, but during this bad time, he hardly came to the reserve at all. He had to make his rounds with a horse and buggy and he travelled for miles in all directions out of Vanderhoof during the epidemic. Father Coccola, who lived on the reserve at that time, knew quite a bit about medicine, and as long as the flu lasted, he moved from cabin to cabin in the village, helping to care for the sick and dying.

The people of the village said that it seemed to be a matter of luck whether you lived or died. Some of the weakest survived and some of the strongest found their way to the village cemetery.

That cemetery—one of the things which filled me with horror during this time was the mass burial. When the epidemic was at its worst, a number of people died within two or three days of each other, and those who were left were too sick to lay out the corpses and make coffins. A large hole was dug in the cemetery, and seven bodies were carefully wrapped and buried side by side.

Many years later, some of my children were working with me at the cemetery. There were old boards scattered around, crosses which had collapsed over the years. I told the young people to gather up the old wood and put it in a pile for burning outside the graveyard fence. Then I noticed that the place where the seven people had been buried so many years ago was now a big hole and that the ground around the spot was very uneven.

I said to my children, "We should get a backhoe and make the ground level." And I told them about the mass burial.

They looked at me and one of them said, "Oh, that's gross!"

Finally the epidemic was over. The bell stopped ringing, and once again my mother and my stepfather were busy with fish and hides and berries. Life was good again.

After being a single child in my grandmother's home,

disowned by my real father, I now found myself with a stepfather, a stepsister, and a baby brother. Perhaps best of all, I was
with my mother. And in the same village, I could see my
Grandmother Ann whenever I wished—she had married the
son of the hereditary chief.

I loved my stepfather. Johnny Paul was about ten years
older than my mother and when he married my mother he
was a widower with a daughter, Bella, who was just my age.
Looking back now, I realize that it was a marriage of oppo-
sites. Johnny was loud, loud—you always knew when he was
around! My mother was different. She was quiet and even-
tempered. I never remember her being cranky or irritated or
annoyed about anything. She didn't talk very much.

How I wish now that my mother and I had talked more to
each other! But that's the way things were, and wishing now
doesn't change anything—she was a woman of few words and
I was like the other children, only interested in the day-to-day
happenings around me. And yet, I know that I was closer to
my quiet mother than to anyone else in the world.

Johnny Paul was one of the best trappers and hunters in the
village. He was a good provider and would do anything to
keep food on the table. He cut firewood for the people of
Vanderhoof, he cleared land, and he acted as an auxiliary
policeman sometimes, travelling to Prince Rupert and Bella
Coola and south into the Caribou.

Looking back now, the thing for which I remember him
best is that he never made any difference between me and his
own daughter Bella. If Bella got a hair ribbon, so did I. From
the day he married my mother, he accepted me as his daughter. Of course, I knew that he was not my father, that I had no
father.

Nowadays, my situation would not be unusual, but in the
years when I was growing up, I don't believe there were other
illegitimate children in our village. Some of the boys and girls
teased me unmercifully about my father. One girl in particu-

lar, older than me, would follow me around calling, "Who's your father? Who's your father?" And then she would shout, "Charlie Pinker! Charlie Pinker!"

That was the only bad thing in those very early years of my life—some of the village people, especially the children, treated me as a person apart, different in some way from themselves. But never Johnny! Never!

———

The village of Stoney Creek was my world and I loved it. I loved the log houses all set out in rows and the little hillocks and the creek which ran through the village. Without that creek, the elders said, there would have been no village, for that was where the fish spawned. Years before, the Indians had lived further along Nulki Lake, but around 1890, families moved to the rolling land through which the creek flowed. In those years, fish was the staple in our diet, and wherever the fish were, there you would find the Natives.

Our day-to-day life, what we did, where we were located, the food we ate, all of these things depended on the season.

In the summer we were in Stoney Creek village. Oh, the village in the hot months of summer was an active place! Berries were picked and fish were caught. The men and women, and the children too, were busy with drying and canning and smoking. This work would go on throughout the daylight hours, and sometimes into the night—our central British Columbian winters were harsh and a family's survival depended on a good store of food laid up for the months ahead.

My role in the family was established when I was still very young. I looked after Mark and the babies who came after him, and wherever we were, I spent much of my time indoors, looking after our home. Johnny, my grandmother, the elders, all used to say, "Mary is a real little mother!" Bella, my stepsister, worked with my mother and learned early to treat hides, to dry and smoke fish, to trap and shoot and do all the things which Native women have done for centuries, and which were so necessary for their families' survival. I had to learn these things when I was much older

But it wasn't all work. Once or twice during the summer, Johnny would harness the horses and we would jump into the wagon and travel to Vanderhoof, nine miles away.

How exciting it was when the horses reached the top of the hill and we could look down on Vanderhoof with its sidewalks and buildings! Johnny drove the team of horses to the edge of town and, in amongst the willows, he tied the horses on a long rope so that they could graze.

When the horses were settled, Bella and I helped my mother to gather kindling for a campfire. We always had a campfire when we went to town—in those days there were no signs telling us that campfires were prohibited! Besides, we had no money to spend in a restaurant, and even if our pockets had been full of dollar bills, we weren't allowed to enter any of the cafés in Vanderhoof. Natives knew that if they walked into a restaurant, they would be asked to leave, and if they refused, the police would be called. When I was a little girl, this didn't bother me—I wouldn't have traded the campfire and the willows and the sounds of the horses grazing for the most expensive dining room in the world!

When the campfire was ablaze, my mother put a kettle on to boil water for tea. She spread a tarp in the shade, and then we all went into the town. Sometimes we did nothing but walk along the wooden sidewalks, looking into the store windows and imagining what we would buy if we had money. Sometimes, if my mother had a little spare cash, we might buy a loaf of store bread—that was a great treat for us—or some goodies from the bakery. Then we would go back to the campfire in amongst the willows and have our tea and treats. Sometimes we'd stay there until dark, driving home to Stoney Creek when the stars were out and the heat of the day was done.

I loved those trips to town! Tea never tasted so good as it did there on the edge of town, with our campfire burning and the horses snorting and grunting as they grazed in the long grass, with my mother and Johnny and Bella and Mark on the tarp beside me, our teacups steaming in our hands.

When I was a little girl, I believe I thought that the long hot days of summer would last forever. Then suddenly—as I grew older I came to know that it would happen but in those early years it was always a surprise to me—there was the first frost early in September and with it, the village emptied of people. One by one the families loaded their wagons with tents and bedding and supplies, and left for their hereditary hunting grounds.

And the village was silent.

CHAPTER THREE

THE FIRST FROST IN SEPTEMBER—that was when we left Stoney Creek. We packed the wagon with a tent and bedding, with guns and shells, tarps and nets; between these things and our family, the wagon couldn't hold another thing! Johnny closed the door of our cabin behind him, shouted "Guuph!" to the horses, and as we drove out of the village, we waved goodbye and called out "See you at Christmas!" to the few people left on the reserve.

We were on our way to Johnny's hereditary hunting grounds at Cluculz Lake, twenty miles east of our village. How Bella and I looked forward to the trip to our hunting grounds! At that time of year, although the mornings were frosty, the sun still held much of its summer warmth, and we loved to feel its heat on our bare arms as we jogged along in the overcrowded wagon, riding through the bush on a narrow trail.

There was so much to see. A moose ran awkwardly in front of our horses for a few minutes before going off into the trees, and there were more deer than we could count grazing along the side of the trail. Mother bears and their cubs looked at us from the edge of the forest before disappearing into the undergrowth. We saw a quick sliding movement, and tried to guess if the shadow we had seen was a fox or a coyote. In the little creeks we passed, we saw beaver dams. The ponds and sloughs had flocks of ducks and Canada geese and all day long birds called from the nearby trees or flew in circles over our heads. The crows, then as now, were everywhere.

When I was a small girl, the land, the rivers and creeks and lakes, were full of life—birds and animals of all kinds were as much a part of the landscape as trees and clouds and sun. Now I can travel five hundred miles in any direction from our village and not see so much as a field mouse. I think with sadness of those trips to the hunting grounds when I was a child and I remember our land as it used to be.

We sometimes camped out one night on our journey to the hunting grounds, and if this happened it was the highlight of the trip. What a rush there was to set up camp! The tent, big pieces of canvas sewn together on a treadle sewing machine, was put up, and spruce boughs were spread on the ground inside the tent to keep the dampness out of the bedding. Mattresses filled with feathers from ducks and geese were placed over the boughs; patchwork quilts, made by my mother and grandmother in the long winter evenings, were our covering at night.

When the tent was up, Johnny went into the woods with his gun; if he was lucky, there would be roast grouse or rabbit stew for supper. Bella and I gathered wood and started the campfire, while my mother dipped into the kitchen box.

That kitchen box—every Native family had one. It was made out of wood, with moose skin hinges and handles, and it went everywhere with us. It held our dishes and pots and pans, and the staples we would need on the road: flour, tea, salt, dried fish, rice. Nowadays, people are cautioned never to leave home without their credit cards. In my day, the last thing we did before we left on a journey was to make sure that our kitchen box was in the wagon with us.

The next day, we set up a more permanent camp on the edge of Cluculz Lake. This was Johnny's hunting grounds, our home for the next five or six weeks. The tent was put up again and nearby, Johnny built a drying rack. He set up poles and put a tarp over them, and every day when fish were netted and deer and moose were shot, it was under this tarp that the food supply for the coming months was prepared.

Once the camp was liveable, the real work started. Johnny was out every day with his gun, tramping the woods on silent feet, tracking the large animals with the skill which made him one of the best hunters in Central British Columbia. Bella and my mother were never still, drying or canning fish and meat, and working with moose and deer hides. It was these same hides which would be turned into mitts and moccasins and jackets for the family. The soaking and scraping and oiling of the hides—this went on for hours each day.

I was the housekeeper. I looked after Mark, kept the fires going and, young as I was, I helped to prepare the meals. Johnny would come in after a day in the bush and say, "You are a real little mother!" That was reward enough for me.

Every day was the same. The only changes in our lives were the weather, and a shortening in the hours of daylight.

And yet, despite the monotony and the mercury in the thermometer which continued to drop each day, I felt sad to leave our camp on the edge of the lake in early October. Sad, yes, but Bella and I were excited too. We were on our way to our next destination, the trapline at Wedgewood, a few miles from Cluculz Lake. It would be in Wedgewood on the bank of the Nechako River that we would spend the winter, only returning to our village for the Christmas holidays.

To see our log cabin at Wedgewood was like seeing an old

friend. It was smaller than our cabin on the reserve—Johnny
said it was sixteen by twenty feet—but it had the same kind of
furniture, homemade table and beds, and a B.C. stove. Oh, it
was snug and warm after those last few nights in the tent at
Cluculz Lake!

It was so quiet in Wedgewood. The family was alone. The
only noises I heard were the wind in the trees and the wild
animals snuffling around our cabin in the night—that and the
trains. Wedgewood was on a branch line of the Canadian
National Railway which ran from Jasper in Alberta to Prince
Rupert on the Pacific Ocean. The railway tracks were very
close to our cabin and several times a day a train rushed past.
I loved the sound of the train. Often at night, I'd go to sleep
thinking about the three stations the train had to pass before it
reached Vanderhoof. It was fun to imagine the farms and the
little railway stations and the towns along the railway tracks,
all the way to the Pacific Ocean.

Then it seemed strange to picture Stoney Creek Reserve,
with the log buildings closed, and the chief and the grown-ups
and the children sleeping in cabins like ours on their traplines
all up and down the Nechako River and along Fraser Lake
and Stuart Lake.

Wedgewood was a happy place for me but I knew, young
as I was, that it was heavy hard work for my mother and
Johnny. Each of them had traplines which stretched across the
Nechako river to Saxon Lake and beyond. Every day, whatever the weather, they had to walk miles, often accompanied
by Bella, to look at their traps, and to empty them of coyotes
and foxes or, if they were lucky, a lynx. That was only the
beginning of their labour. The carcasses, often frozen, had to
be brought back to the cabin, skinned, and the pelts scraped
and stretched. Each morning, even if the weather was bitter or
my parents were tired from their work of the day before, they
would have to go out on their rounds again.

I never heard them complain. They were young and tough and had been accustomed to life on the trapline almost from their infancy.

Sometimes a weasel or a muskrat was caught in one of their traps, and when this happened they gave the little animal to me. I watched my mother and Johnny preparing the pelts of bigger animals, and before very long I was able to skin and stretch a pelt of my own. Soon my mother showed me how to set out a trapline around our cabin to catch some of the smaller animals which came exploring or looking for food. On the mornings when I found a weasel in one of my traps, I was happy for the rest of the day.

Even as children we knew that the work at Stoney Creek in the summer and the hunting and fishing in September at Cluculz Lake meant food for the family. The trapline was different. The skins were sold, and it was this money which provided the family with clothing and flour and sugar and tea.

Everything we did, the places in which we lived—all, all were important to the survival of our family. I understood that this was so.

Before I quite knew it, we were preparing to return to the reserve for Christmas. We counted off the days as December 25th approached. We had so many reasons for our excitement. We knew that the villagers would be back in Stoney Creek for the holidays, and that our relatives would be coming from other reserves to celebrate with us. We looked forward to the visiting and feasting and dancing. And then there were the pelts—Bella and I had our little parcels of furs for which we would receive money from the fur buyer in Vanderhoof. I wasted hours dreaming about all that I would do with my few dollars. Weasel pelts didn't bring in much money in those days. I didn't mind; even a dollar represented a fortune to me.

When the day of our departure finally arrived, Johnny arranged for the horses to be cared for by the section foreman at Wedgewood, the furs were stacked neatly on the station platform waiting for the train to be flagged down—I clutched my own small parcel of furs tightly in my hand—and then we were on the train, on our way to Vanderhoof.

Our first stop in Vanderhoof was to the shop of the fur buyer, where we passed over our pelts and the man behind the counter calculated what he owed us. As soon as Bella and I were paid out, we flew out of the shop and into the general store as fast as our legs would carry us. Candy, gum, a pair of mitts, an undershirt—our small fortunes were soon gone!

We had no Christmas tree, no presents, no turkey or mince pies—these things were not part of our Christmas on the reserve. And yet everyone was happy. Families had returned from their traplines, and relatives from Fort George and Fort St. James and all the reserves around were visiting in every cabin. Our cabin seemed to be always full of people and noise; there was laughter, and talk of the weather and the price of fur and the news about births and weddings and sickness and death. How strange it was to hear so much sound after the quiet of Wedgewood! A few days before, the village had been empty. Now, everyone was back.

On Christmas Eve, I walked with my family through the frosty night to the church. All the villagers and their relatives were there. We had no missionary to say Mass, but the church had been heated and, just before midnight, everyone knelt down and prayed together. The church was so crowded that it seemed there was not room for one more body, and no wonder—in our village it was considered a very bad thing not to be praying in the church on Christmas Eve. My grandmother told me that there had been other Christmases when a missionary was living on the reserve and then a beautiful Midnight Mass was held.

And what dances Bella and I attended! Every few nights,

one or other of the villagers passed the word around that there would be a dance in his cabin that night. All the furniture, the homemade tables and benches and beds, were moved outside in the snow, and to the music of a fiddle everyone danced, even the very old. The cabins were small and crowded but somehow everyone managed to step to the music, even children as young as Bella and me. Sometime during the dance the door would be flung open to cool off overheated dancers, and the heat of the cabin would form steam when it met the frigid air outside.

That's what it was like—music and laughter and steam pouring through the open door.

———————

A few days after the new year had begun, the villagers and their visitors scattered back to their traplines across Central British Columbia. Once again we caught the train, this time back to Wedgewood, back to the stillness, the hard work, the sounds of animals and wind and speeding trains in the night.

And once again, our village was silent.

Carrier Natives at Fort St. James. (*Provincial Archives of B.C.* *#10824*)

Carrier Natives drying Kokanee fish. (*Provincial Archives of B.C.* *#94842*)

Berrying at Nulki Lake (*Provincial Archives of B.C. #96776*)

A Carrier family in 1912. (*Provincial Archives of B.C. #96809*)

Mary John (right) at the age of 14 in 1927.

Mary John's in-laws—the parents of Lazare John.

Two of Mary's daughters in 1947: Shirley (left), and Helen.

Mary's half-brother, Mark (Chapter 14).

Mary John in 1987.

CHAPTER FOUR

ONE DAY IN LATE AUGUST IN THE YEAR 1920, when I was two months past my seventh birthday, my mother called me into our cabin on the reserve.

"Mary," she said, "tomorrow you are going to school."

School? What was school? I didn't know.

It didn't occur to me to ask my mother what this thing called school might be. Native children were raised to accept the statements of their parents and elders, and to ask no questions. When I was young and decisions were made for me by my parents or the elders—attending school, going to work, getting married—I obeyed them as I had been taught to do.

So I went to bed that night in August, 1920, with the question, still unanswered, going through my head . . . what is school?

The next day, Mary Sutherland and I—she was just my age and in years to come, we became each other's aunt, as she married my uncle and I married hers—climbed into Mr. Bloomfield's wagon with two other children from Stoney

Creek. I waved goodbye to my mother and Johnny and Bella and Mark. I waved to my Grandmother Ann and I saw that she was crying. Why was she crying? I didn't know. I didn't know where this wagon was taking us, or who Mr. Bloomfield was, or how long I would be away from the village.

Aunt Mary knew no more than I did. Nobody had told us anything.

I was confused as the wagon rolled out of the village towards Vanderhoof, but I was excited too. My mother had given me twenty-five cents just before I climbed into the wagon and told me that I could buy some candy. We went first to the railway station in Vanderhoof where we picked up two nuns and some boys who had come in on the morning train. Mr. Bloomfield stopped just long enough in the town to let me buy a large bag of mixed candy and then we were off again. I did not know where we were going but I could tell from our direction that we were not going back to my village. We were moving north.

When the novelty of the bag of candy had worn off, I found myself listening to the older girls in the wagon who spoke my language. They talked about the Mission School and Fort St. James. I understood from what they said that this Mission School was a big building, where many children learned to read and write and to speak English.

I finally found the courage to ask, "How many days will it take to learn to speak English and to read and write?" I was told that to learn such things took many years.

From that moment, I was homesick. I was frightened too. Many years . . . did that mean I would not see my family or my village for years and years? I knew that Fort St. James was many miles from my home. I had relatives there and I had heard them say that they could not come to Stoney Creek often because of the distance. Suddenly this going to school was a very terrible thing that was happening to me.

That night we camped in a field about half way between

Vanderhoof and Fort St. James. The boys put up a tent and Aunt Mary and I and the two nuns slept in it. Although I was sleeping with one of the nuns, I was very cold in the night. Towards dawn I thought about the boys and Mr. Bloomfield. They were sleeping in the wagon. Are they very cold? I wondered.

Late the next day, we crossed the river on a ferry, passed through the village of Fort St. James, and there, on the edge of Stuart Lake, was the church and the Mission School.

Many years passed before I learned the history of the Mission School. It was started by missionaries, the Oblates of Mary Immaculate, years before I went there in 1920, although the dormitories which allowed the school to take in boarders were built just three years before my first year in the school. The work of the school, the teaching, cooking, laundry and cleaning, all of this was done by the pupils and four nuns. These nuns belonged to the Sisters of Child Jesus, an order which was started in rural France. The sisters were trained for menial duties only and, I'm sure, had never expected to end up as teachers in the wilds of British Columbia!

The first problem the sisters and missionaries had to face was that the new pupils spoke only their Native language. I had hardly heard English spoken before I went to the Mission School. The problem was solved by putting the new pupils, no matter what their ages, into the first grade on their arrival at the school in order to teach them English.

When I went there with Mary Sutherland, I had no idea that my village was opposed to this school. The Native parents missed their children and knew that their children were unhappy away from home. They did not like the strict discipline practised by the nuns and missionaries, and they felt that their children were not fed and looked after as they would have been at home.

I did not know that three years before I went to the Mission School, the Stoney Creek Council, pressed by the mothers of the village, had sent a telegram to the government in

Ottawa which said that the people wanted a school on their
own reserve. "This Indian village has ninety-five school age
children . . . we can feed our children at home then," said the
telegram. Nor did I know that later, the Native people were
forced to apologize for sending that telegram.

Another thing I didn't know was that the Oblates were
equally dissatisfied with the school. The missionaries felt that
the school was too close to Fort St. James village and to the
Necoslie Reserve. How could they teach the children to speak
English, they asked, how could the children be trained prop-
erly, if the parents were constantly interfering? Besides, the
aim of the Oblates was to teach the Native children to become
farmers and farmers' wives, and there was not enough land
around the school to provide that training. No, the missionaries were not happy about the Mission School. . . .

I knew none of these things. I only knew that I was always
homesick.

Mary Sutherland and I used to look across the lake and
think that on the other side, many miles away, our families
were netting, cleaning and drying fish in the village, travelling
to the hunting grounds, or walking along their traplines. I
could picture so clearly the drying rack at Cluculz Lake and
the cabin at Wedgewood. At night I would try to remember
how the trains sounded in the darkness as they rushed past the
little Wedgewood station.

Just once, my mother and Johnny phoned me. I couldn't
believe that I was hearing their voices, that they actually stood
at the other end of miles and miles of telephone wire. Oh, I
cried silently, if I could only see them! I believe that I thought
I would never never be with them again.

Christmas was the worst. Many of the pupils who lived on
the Necoslie Reserve in Fort St. James were able to spend the
Christmas holidays with their parents, but Mary's and mine
lived too far away—there was no money to have us brought
home, so we stayed in the school. I thought about all the

people who would be coming back to Stoney Creek. I couldn't stop thinking about the dances and the visiting and the walk through frosty darkness to the little church on Christmas Eve. I thought I would die, I was so lonesome for my parents and my village.

Mary and I cried all through the Christmas holidays. Nothing the nuns or the missionaries did could make us feel any better.

"I'm always hungry," said Mary.

"So am I," I said.

We did not say this in our own language, but in the halting English which we were slowly learning. The nuns and the priest who was the principal had warned all of us that it was forbidden to speak the Indian language, and that if we broke this rule, we would be punished. I suppose they believed that without such a rule, we little savages would never learn a civilized language! We were deathly afraid of being whipped. Even when we were alone, Mary and I tried to remember to speak in the new language.

We saw so many pupils whipped for speaking their Native language or running away or stealing food. The boys were thrashed for speaking to the girls, and the girls were thrashed for writing notes to the boys.

Mary and I were terrified when we saw someone being whipped. We said to each other—in English—"This is not a thing our parents do to us." So even when we talked of our hunger, we did not use our Native language.

I was always hungry. I missed the roast moose, the dried beaver meat, the fish fresh from a frying pan, the warm bread and bannock and berries. Oh, how I missed the food I used to have in my own home!

At school, it was porridge, porridge, porridge, and if it wasn't that, it was boiled barley or beans, and thick slices of bread spread with lard. Weeks went by without a taste of meat or fish. Such things as sugar or butter or jam only appeared on our tables on feast days, and sometimes not even then. A few times, I would catch the smell of roasting meat coming from the nuns' dining room, and I couldn't help myself—I would follow that smell to the very door.

Apart from the summers, I believe I was hungry for all seven of the years I was at school. Only later did I learn that the government gave the missionaries $125 each year for every pupil in the school. This had to cover our food and clothing for ten months of the year, in addition to running and maintaining the school. No wonder we were on rations more suited to a concentration camp!

I had dreamed of going home so often that when, early in July of 1921, Mary and I tumbled into Mr. Bloomfield's wagon, I couldn't believe it was really happening. We hugged each other.

"We're going home!" we said to each other in our own language. "We're going home to Stoney Creek!"

Everyone cried when the wagon stopped and we were on Stoney Creek land once more. My mother and grandmother, Bella and Mark—everyone cried at the sight of us, two little girls, now eight years old, who had been away so long.

And yes, there were the log cabins and the smoke shacks and the creek and the little church, and Johnny standing behind my mother with a big grin on his face, just as I had remembered them. Nothing had changed! The loudest wails came from Mary Sutherland and me. I think that was the happiest day of my life.

In September, when Mr. Bloomfield came with his wagon to take us back to the Mission School, we all cried again. And the loudest cries . . . they came from Mary and me.

CHAPTER FIVE

IF YOU DRIVE WEST FROM THE TOWN of Vanderhoof along the highway towards Prince Rupert, through the village of Fort Fraser, and continue in a westerly direction for a few miles, you will see a large brick building set on the southern shore of Fraser Lake. Even from the highway you will notice that the building is closed, its doors barred, its windows boarded up. The fields are overgrown with grass and weeds, the outbuildings are tumbling down, the small graveyard is untended.

When I see it now, it is hard to remember the excitement that the people of Stoney Creek village felt in 1921 and 1922 when that brick building was under construction and a section of land was being cleared of trees. We were told that the Mission School in Fort St. James was going to be closed, and that all the students would be attending this new school, Lejac, soon to be completed on the shore of Fraser Lake. Everyone talked about the new school.

"It has two wings, one for the girls and one for the boys.

Each wing has four dormitories, and there is a big washroom in each dormitory," said one.

"You should see the size of the dining room," said another.

"And, oh, the kitchen—and the sewing room, and the recreation halls, and the little chapel, and there is even a hospital and a visiting room for parents of the pupils!"

"And there will be a big garden so that our children will get nice fresh vegetables—and a barn and piggery, which means milk and good meat. Oh! Oh! Oh!"

Many of the men from my village were helping to build the new school. They kept the excitement alive with their stories of the modern wonders which were going into the building of Lejac—I think some of us expected to see a Buckingham Palace rising on the shore of Fraser Lake!

In February of 1922, the students, like Mary Sutherland and I who were in the Mission School, the teachers and staff, all were transferred to Lejac. That was quite a move! Several teams of horses and sleighs loaded with children made the trip from Fort St. James to Vanderhoof. We waited in the Nechako Hotel for the train that would take us on to Lejac. As we travelled towards Lejac, I told myself that now everything would be different.

The first sight of the large brick school brought gasps from us. It's so big, I thought.

Everyone raced to be the first into the building and once in, we ran from room to room, turning water taps on and off and flushing the toilets. We peeked into the sewing room and the chapel. The hospital—that was a slight disappointment, with its bare walls, its few cots, and large cupboards. We very soon learned to call it the infirmary. But everything else was so new, so big. Shouts of, "Come here! Look at this!" sounded through the building.

I found it hard to go to sleep that first night in Lejac. What wonders, I thought as I drifted off to sleep, would the next day hold?

When a large plate of porridge was served for breakfast the next morning, I had my first warning that despite the modern building, nothing had changed.

The pupils were separated according to sex as rigidly as they had been in the old Mission School. They were segregated in the classroom, the play areas, the chapel, the dining room. The nuns and missionaries were determined that the boys and girls—even those related to each other—should be kept apart. On my second day in Lejac, a boy was whipped in front of the whole school because he had wet his bed the night before. Soon after, the first girl was beaten for dropping a note near a boy's desk. In the first week, three boys ran away. They were brought back by the Mounties and thrashed in front of the whole school. The Indian language was forbidden as it had been in Fort St. James, and any student who broke this rule was punished.

By the end of the first day I was hungry. Within hours of coming to Lejac, I was as homesick as I had been in the Mission School. Except for Sunday, our routine was always the same.

I would tumble out of bed early in the morning and wash in a hurry. When my bed was made, I ran to chapel and attended Mass. It seemed to go on forever, but when it was done, it was time to go to the girls' side of the dining room for a plate of porridge. I hated porridge more than anything! Oh, I used to think, if I could only have milk and brown sugar with it, like we have for breakfast at home!

After breakfast there were chores—sometimes it was clearing the table or sweeping or dusting. When our chores were done, it was time for class.

The afternoon was just like the morning. Lunch was a plate of boiled barley or beans and a thick slice of bread spread with lard. The only time we had butter on our bread was on a feast day. After lunch, we had chores and class again. The afternoon finished with a sewing or singing lesson.

At seven-thirty in the evening, there was Benediction in the chapel, and at eight-thirty, in total silence, the students went to their dormitories, said their prayers and fell into bed.

I found that I wanted to learn. I liked to read; I even liked arithmetic and spelling. Sometimes I found myself wishing that we did more studying. I said this once to an older girl.

"I wish," I whispered, "that we were learning more things out of books."

I remember that she looked at me as if I was crazy.

We spent a lot of time changing clothes. We had clothes for chapel, clothes for work, clothes for play, clothes for class. I felt that my life was a continual round of getting out of one set of clothing and into another—and heaven help the student who was wearing play clothes in chapel or work clothes in class!

I knew that my life in Lejac was plain sailing compared with many of the other students. I was shy and naturally submissive. The older students sometimes called me Teacher's Pet, and although I did not like this name, I knew that it was true. I was teacher's pet.

I was scared of breaking a rule and being punished for it. I never used my Native language except very privately and in a whisper, I never spoke to a boy, and the only thing I had ever stolen was the sugar at the bottom of tea cups when I was cleaning up the nuns' dining room table. I would run my fingers around the bottom of the cups and then suck the sugar off them. Oh, that sugar, brown with the tea and hardened slightly, was good!

And another thing—the teachers thought that I had one of the best singing voices in the school, and very often, when other girls were out pulling up roots from the land that was being cleared, I was inside having a singing lesson. I didn't miss all of the outside work, but unlike some of the other girls, at least I missed some of it.

So much of the work in Lejac was hard, especially for the

boys. The bigger ones spent almost no time in class. Instead, they were cutting down trees and pulling up stumps, or else they were up before daylight feeding the horses and milking the cows. Long after he left Lejac one boy said, "I'm just a human bulldozer!" and that described exactly the work they did. There was no machinery of any kind, especially in the very early years; everything had to be done by brute physical force.

The boys often rebelled and I didn't blame them. They were supposed to be in Lejac to get educated, but instead they were unpaid labourers, living on poor food and with no more freedom than if they were prisoners in a jail. When the principal explained to them that they were being trained to be agricultural workers, the boys laughed.

"Imagine trying to turn an Indian into a farmer!" they said.

Time after time, the boys ran away. Some were successful and managed to reach their parents' traplines, but more often, they were caught by the Mounties, brought back and whipped. Some years after I was in the school, four boys ran away from Lejac in the dead of winter. They died of exposure before they could reach their reserves.

The girls did less hard physical labour than the boys, but in many ways, our time in Lejac was just as hard. Except when we were outside pulling up roots which lay on the surface of the ground after the land was cleared, we were always inside, under the watchful eye of a teacher. It seemed to bother them to see us idle—every time we finished a task, a piece of rough cloth and a needle were put in our hands with the order "Sew!" We made all of the dresses and uniforms worn in the school, and socks, drawers, chemises, and aprons.

When the boys worked outside in groups, the teachers did not find it easy to watch them. With the girls it was different. We had no privacy in our lives except when we went the bathroom, and sometimes, not even there!

I feel sad now when I remember how excited we all were to go to Lejac in 1922, when I remember the hopes we had that it would be a happier place than the Mission School, and especially when I remember how fast our hopes died. Nothing was changed except that we were in a bigger building with more modern conveniences, and that there was more work expected of us, sometimes very hard work.

The food was no better than it had been in the Mission School. We were always hungry. The braver or more desperate ones who stole food out of the pantry were continually caught and punished, just as they had been in Fort St. James. Driven by hunger, despite brutal thrashings, many of the pupils continued to steal food. I didn't blame them—many times, I was tempted to steal a piece of meat or a cookie from the staff dining room myself.

We had hoped that with the parlor set aside for visitors, we would see more of our families. This was not to be. The room itself was small, and very soon became known as the Indian Parlor. My parents could not afford to come for a visit, but even if they had had the money for such a trip, they would have been allowed to stay for only two and one-half hours.

I did not realize until I was an adult and away from Lejac that the school must have been as big a disappointment to the missionaries and nuns as it was to us. The school was still getting only $125 a year for each student from the federal government in Ottawa, and in the bigger school, expenses were higher. I know now that the Oblates were always trying to make one dollar do the work of two.

Added to that, the parents were no more supportive of Lejac than they had been of the Mission School in Fort St. James. They complained of the food, the work, the punishments. They wanted schools on their own reserves, and nothing less would satisfy them. They wanted their children at home with them.

And within the school itself, the missionaries and the nuns

had to deal with one hundred and eighty Native children who were always hungry, always homesick. The boys were openly rebellious, many of them stealing or running away or getting the girls off in some corner alone with them. Unlike the boys, the female students were seldom openly rebellious. Instead, they were sullen and depressed.

Lejac was not a happy place.

CHAPTER SIX

IN THE FIVE YEARS THAT I attended school in Lejac, some things were harder, some easier to bear.

When the first of May came, when the ice was off the lake and the buds on the trees had turned into clean green leaves, I would say to myself, "Soon I will be going back to my village."

And as the hot days of summer dwindled away, I would know that my time in the village was nearly over for another year, and every morning when I opened my eyes, I would think, "I don't know how I can go back to Lejac."

I was growing up.

In earlier years, when I had to go back to school, there was always a terrible fear that I would never see my family again . . . that this time, I was being taken away forever. And in the summers, when I was younger, it never occurred to me that one day a wagon or truck would come for me and I would have to leave my family again. Summer seemed endless in those days and I could not imagine that it would ever end.

Later, as I grew older, the awful fear of losing my family

and my village was gone; even as the truck drove into the village to collect the students, I knew that I would see my parents again in ten months. But I also learned that summer was not endless, and that one day I would have to climb into a vehicle and again be taken away.

In the five years that I attended Lejac, it never became easier to leave home.

School life did not change. Year after year, there was the work, the punishments, the boredom, the terrible food, the changing from work clothes to uniform to play clothes and then into uniform and work clothes again.

Even then, I knew that there were also some good things about school. I could now speak English, and I was making what the teachers called excellent progress in reading, writing, and arithmetic. I had also learned other, more practical things: sewing, cooking, and the other domestic skills which the nuns and missionaries hoped would turn girls like me into good farmers' wives. Sister Superior gave me singing lessons each day, and while the lessons were going on, I was as happy as I could be away from my village.

And sometimes there was a break in the routine. Two or three times each year, on a warm day, the students would walk to Robinson Point on the shore of Fraser Lake. How we looked forward to these breaks! At Robinson Point we would swim and have a picnic. Those days were highlights in the year. The sun was hot, the water cool, and the freedom to run and jump and shout, especially for the girls, left us feeling happy for days afterwards.

Sometimes on feast days there would be stew and bread spread with butter, instead of boiled barley or porridge or beans. The stew was rich with meat and carrots and potatoes, and on those days, I would think that I had never tasted such delicious food.

One time in the fall, I remember, an old lady, Mrs. Francois, was fishing for whitefish in Fraser Lake, just below Lejac. She caught many more fish than she could use. She smoked several dozen of them and sold them to Father Coccola, who was principal of Lejac at the time. The nuns had never cooked smoked fish, so the older Native girls made dinner that day—they had cooked smoked fish many times in the summer on their own reserves. They split the whitefish in half and baked the pieces in the oven. Each of us was served half a fish and a potato.

For many days after this treat, we followed Father Coccola around, asking him, "Father, when will you buy more fish?"

Father Coccola always replied, "When I have some money!"

Sad to say, he never did have money for such a treat again.

One of the chores I was assigned in later years which I both liked and dreaded was going for the mail. Mr. and Mrs. Allan, who operated the post office, lived across the boys' playground in a small building. Mr. Allan was an engineer and his wife taught music in our school. I had to pick up the mail each day, and I would have enjoyed my daily visit with what was to me contact with the outside world except for one thing—I had to cross the boys' playground both going to the post office and coming back again. How I dreaded the jeers and calls from the boys! "Felix is your boyfriend!" or "Ernie loves Mary!" or "Johnny wants to kiss you!"

I would run like a rabbit across the playground, trying to shut my ears to those teasing voices. I would make my visit with Mr. and Mrs. Allan last as long as I could; I knew that those same boys would be waiting for me on my return trip to the school. The last thing I wanted was to be close enough to boys to listen to their teasing!

———

It was impossible, even in the summer, to forget Lejac. Delegations of parents went to the chief each August and asked him, "Why do our children have to go away from us in September? Why can't we have a day school here?"

The chief would say, "Tell me what is the matter with Lejac? Why are you coming to me every summer with this request?"

"We miss our children," the parents would say. "They go away for ten months, and when they come back, they have grown so much we hardly know them. They are forgetting their Carrier language. The boys are not learning how to hunt and trap and set a net for fish—no, they are learning how to milk a cow and plow a field! They are supposed to go to Lejac to be educated, but they are not in the classrooms. They are in the fields or the barns, and the girls are too much in the sewing room or the kitchen. The work is too hard for them. It is said by many that the teachers are not really teachers at all. They are not trained as the teachers are in the school in Vanderhoof. And if our children complain or run away, they are whipped. This is not the Carrier way."

"Stop! Stop!" the chief would say. "I will talk to Father Coccola. I will talk to the government man."

A few days later, the chief would meet with the villagers again. And he would say, "The government man says he gives $125 each year for every student. This is given to the school and the government man says he has no more money to give."

The Natives would say, "Give us the $125 for each student and we will have our own day school. Then our children will be with us and they will learn the Carrier ways."

The chief would continue, "Father Coccola says that if the children stayed here, they would not go to school. They would go with their parents to the hunting grounds and the traplines."

"No! No! We would send our children to school!"

"And Father Coccola says that it is very hard to run the school when parents do not support it. He says the first principal, Father Allard, suffered a nervous breakdown and had to leave. And the second principal, Father Wolfe, only stayed a few months. Now we have Father Coccola. He says the students are forbidden to speak Carrier because, if they were allowed, they would never learn to speak English. He says that the students are only punished when they do very bad things—when they steal or lie or when they run away. He says they must be punished when they try to run away, because what they do is very dangerous. They could get lost and die, or they could freeze to death. He says the school is very poor and that is why it does not have teachers who are trained. He says the nuns work very hard. He says everyone must work hard so that things will get better. And that is what Father Coccola says."

Each summer we heard this same talk. And each September, I went back to Lejac, and when I arrived there, I found that nothing had changed.

There was the principal, Father Coccola, whom we hardly ever saw except in chapel. There were the same nuns, some of them young and sorry for the homesick youngsters, some of them old and tired and cross. There was the same serge to be made into uniforms, the same porridge to be eaten, the same whippings to be witnessed, the same rush to change clothes, the same prayers to be said, the same silence at bedtime.

And for me, there was always the same longing to be at home with my family.

CHAPTER SEVEN

IT WAS AUGUST OF 1927, AND ALREADY I was waking every morning with the thought that the summer was nearly over and that I would soon be back in school. And I thought, as I always did on opening my eyes, "I don't know how I can go back to Lejac." And then, there was a very strange happening on the reserve.

One day an old Model T drove into the village. In the car were three men and two women. They said they were doctors and healers from a reserve in the Kootenay area in the southeast section of British Columbia and that they practised medicine in the old Native way. Because they were Natives, and many villagers believed in Native medicine, the people of Stoney Creek trusted them.

I watched as the villagers, some of them my relatives, flocked to the healers. There were people with tuberculosis or arthritis, children whose spines were crippled, young people with twisted bodies who had to be carried to the healers by their parents. I had never seen so many sick and crippled people together in one place in my life; everyone in the village was surprised to see how many Natives needed the help of these healers.

The doctor and his helpers charged some people two dollars, some ten or twenty dollars. When the sick person had handed over the money, the doctor would sing in the Native language, and he would put a bottle against the sick part of the person he was healing. The other healers would lay hands on the patient. After a little time had passed, the doctor would show the onlookers the bottle—where before he said it had been empty, now it had many bugs in it.

"See, see how I have taken the sickness out!" he cried.

The Natives of Stoney Creek murmured their amazement as they looked at the bugs in the bottle. Some of them crowded around the doctor and his healers and begged that the bugs be taken out of their wife, their husband, their child.

For three days the healings went on. Then the doctor and his healers jumped in their Model T and left the reserve.

Many people spoke about the wonders that the doctor and his helpers had performed. Everyone was happy. People imagined the village without tuberculosis or arthritis or twisted limbs and spines. It was as if we were celebrating a feast day in the middle of summer.

A few days later, there was no happiness in the village. Many people talked.

"There is no money left in the village," said one.

"All our money was given to that doctor," said another.

"My wife spit blood again today."

"My son still has to be carried—he can't walk. I paid that doctor twenty dollars to make him walk."

"I'll bet the bugs were in the bottle all the time."

"Wait till we tell Father Coccola about this!"

"You had better not tell him, or our children will be punished when they go back to school. The missionaries don't like our medicine."

I listened and I was afraid. Some of my relatives had given money to the Native doctor. I began to shake. I could imagine Sister Superior with the willow switch, standing me up in front of the whole school and thrashing me because my relatives had believed they could be healed in the Carrier way.

I went to my mother. "I am afraid to go back to school. The people in the village say that children of families who went to the healers will be whipped when they go back to Lejac."

My mother talked to my stepfather. That night she said to me, "I need you to help me. You don't go back to Lejac."

I really began to believe that I would never go back to Lejac when, a few days later, we set up camp at Johnny Paul's hunting grounds on the shore of Cluculz Lake. And oh, it was good to be back there again after so many years, to see Johnny and his brother Gus go off with their guns in the morning, to see Bella and my mother drying fish and scraping hides, to have Mark or one of the other little ones call, "Mary, I'm hungry! Can I have something to eat?"

Still, I was afraid that a visitor might come, and every time a twig snapped or the dog barked, I ran to my mother. Each fall, the Mounties called at hunting grounds to pick up students who hadn't returned to Lejac. I knew that Father Coccola would send someone for me. After this small time of freedom and a return to the old days, I felt that I would die if I was taken back to school.

I was not disappointed. When we were at Cluculz Lake two or three days, Constable Bill Manson rode into the camp. I had heard the sound of his horse coming towards us through the bush and I ran to my mother.

"I've come to take Mary back to school," he said.

"I need her to help me," said my mother.

"She has one more year to go to school. Then she can stay with you and help you," said the constable.

"No," my mother said. "I have five little ones and she is the oldest. I won't send her back."

The constable talked to my mother for a few more minutes. She repeated the same thing over and over: "I need her to help me. I won't send her back." Finally the constable shook his head, turned his horse and rode off, back to where he had come from.

When I saw him disappear into the bush, when I couldn't hear the sound of his horse, and the dog had gone back to sleep, then I knew that I was safe. I watched my mother move silently around the camp and I whispered to myself over and over, "Now I will never have to leave my mother again."

CHAPTER EIGHT

NOW CAME THE GOOD YEARS. Again there was summer in the village, fall at Cluculz Lake, winter in our cabin at Wedgewood, with a return to Stoney Creek for Christmas. Once more I could rejoice in our seasonal wanderings. It was as if I was five or six years old again and I could watch the changing of the seasons without fear.

The long hot days of summer with my family seemed endless to me again. Only the time spent in Vanderhoof reminded me of the big world outside of Stoney Creek. Sometimes Johnny and my mother found jobs, clearing land or cutting firewood for sale, on the edge of Vanderhoof. At these times we would spend two or three weeks, surrounded by willows, living in a tent with our campfire burning all day and into the night. The trip to the hunting grounds, sometimes with a stopover on the way, the day-to-day routine of life and work on the edge of the lake, the move to our little cabin at Wedgewood, and the date on the calendar at the beginning of December when Bella and I began to count the days until we travelled back to our village for the Christmas holidays—these things made me feel as if I had found Heaven again!

Once again I was the Little Mother, as Johnny called me.

My mother and Johnny had five children after the birth of my half-brother Mark. Three of them died as very young children, but Mark and Alec and Melanie, all younger than Bella and me, survived. When someone asks me what caused the deaths of my two half-brothers and one half-sister, I have to say, "I don't know." In those days and even later when I was having my own family, children travelled with their parents to the hunting grounds and traplines until they were old enough to go to school. Pneumonia or diptheria or any other infant disease could be fatal. There was no doctor for many many miles—there was only the child's mother, and if she was fortunate, other and older women in the camp, to nurse a sick child.

There must have been sad times in those years after I left Lejac—such things as sickness and death must have occurred in my life. The hard work, the poverty, the isolation from the white world, and the feelings of inferiority this gave us, all these things were a part of my world. And yet, as long as I was with my family in the village or at Cluculz Lake or Wedgewood, the bad moments seemed to pass. The happy moments are the ones I remember now.

One day towards the end of the summer after I left Lejac, I wandered away from the creek where my half-brothers were playing, and entered our log cabin. I was just in time to see my mother packing the kitchen box.

"Where are we going?" I asked.

"To Shelley," said my mother.

I jumped with excitement. "Oh," I said, "I love visiting."

"We're going to a potlatch," said my mother. "Your grandmother's sister is going to have a tombstone placed on her daughter's grave."

Now I was really excited. A potlatch was much better than

just visiting. There would be food and presents and many many people would come to Shelley. I didn't know how I could wait until the next day when our journey would start.

I knew quite a lot about potlatches because the villagers often talked about them. I knew that long ago the government had forbidden the Natives to hold potlatches. I often wondered why the government would do such a bad thing. The villagers said, "The government thought that the Natives were giving too much away and that they were making themselves poor. The Natives weren't giving away—they were sharing. What they gave helped other Natives. We like to share. We like to give gifts. That is the way of our people."

Years ago, said the villagers, because the police used to stop potlatches, many of the Native bands held the gatherings in great secrecy. Now the police didn't seem to care whether potlatches were held or not.

I had often heard about the potlatch that had been held when my stepfather's mother died. Each daughter and daughter-in-law had made four or five hides. The hides were put into the centre of the room when the feasting was done. The clan members cut the hides into moccasin-size squares, and these were given away, along with dried beaver meat. I would have liked to have been at that potlatch.

Shelley! That reserve was many miles away. The people in my village often talked about Shelley, and how the Fort George Band had moved there from the junction of the Fraser and Nechako Rivers, where they had lived for generations. Until my mother married Johnny Paul, the Fort George Band had been our band, and because of this, I liked to listen to the talk about it.

Early in my life I had heard about the move to Shelley. In 1913, the year when I was born, the Fort George Band had sold many hundreds of acres of what is now Prince George to the Grand Trunk Railway. Some of the younger band members were very bitter about this sale. They said that the people had not been paid enough and that they were still waiting for the full amount of the money. These younger people said they had traded valuable land for a few hundred acres out in the bush. They blamed the sale on the federal government in Ottawa and on Father Coccola.

The elders did not agree. They said that Father Coccola was right when he wanted the band moved away from the white man's town, that the young girls were being corrupted and the young men were getting drunk.

But even the elders complained about one thing: they were angry that as soon as the band members were moved from their village to Shelley, the Grand Trunk Railway people had burned the houses in Fort George village to the ground. In doing this, they had desecrated the burial ground, the resting place of our forebears.

I couldn't believe it when I saw five wagons and buggies lined up for the trip to Shelley. So many people going to the potlatch!

We stopped over one night between Stoney Creek and Prince George. I always loved stopovers, and on this trip, because there were so many of us, it was more exciting than usual. The tents were put up, campfires were started and the men went off with their guns and nets. They came back with a deer and many fish, and we feasted all together in a large group.

Another thing I liked about the trip was that, because it was late in August, there were very few insects. This meant that we did not have to set smudge pots inside the tents. I never knew which I hated more, the mosquitoes and black flies, or the smudge pots!

Bella and I were very excited when we came to the top of the hill overlooking Prince George and we could see the town spread out in the valley below us. This was our favorite town.

Everyone knew that unlike Vanderhoof, in Prince George a
Native could go into any restaurant or dining room without
the Mounties being called to throw him out. I often heard the
Stoney Creek people say that Prince George was a good town
for Natives and Vanderhoof was a bad one. Often I found
myself saying this.

Sometimes now, when I come to the top of the hill and see
the city nestling between the two rivers, I remember how
excited my step-sister and I were at our first sight of Prince
George. At other times, I whisper to myself, "All that land
down there once belonged to my people—Connaught Hill
and the park where my ancestors are buried, the city centre
where blocks of businesses now stand, the land where the
trains run, the subdivisions—all this was ours before the government and the church and the railway told us 'Sell! Sell!'"

But on that day so many years ago, on our way to the
potlatch in Shelley, I had no such bitter thoughts.

Our caravan of five buggies and wagons drove through
town and across the railway tracks. When we reached the
Island Cache on the other side of the tracks, we found many
people from Shelley with their tents already in place. They
had come to town for a visit, before the potlatch started.

The next two days in the Island Cache passed all too
quickly. I went from one tent to another with my mother or
my grandmother, visiting relatives and friends. Everyone
seemed to be talking and eating and drinking tea. I thought to
myself, "This is just like Christmas, except that we are in tents
instead of cabins, and there is no snow on the ground."

On the third day, the tents were taken down, the fires were
dampened, and the buggies and wagons made the journey to
Shelley, a few miles away on the Fraser River. The time in
Shelley was even more exciting than the two days in the Island
Cache. We stayed in Shelley for one week.

My grandmother and her friends made what seemed like
mountains of doughnuts and cakes and cookies, and every

night there was a dance. There were men playing violins and guitars, and everyone danced, even the very old and the very young.

On the last day, my grandmother's clan served a big meal to all the people. When the feasting was done, my grandmother's sister gave gifts and souvenirs of her dead daughter to each family that had come to the potlatch. The souvenirs were dishes and clothing and many things which had belonged to her daughter.

That last night, I stayed with a sister of my grandmother's. People liked to tease me because I was so shy, and my grandmother's sister was the biggest tease of them all. In front of many people, she said to me, "I have my trapline set and when you say your prayers tonight, Mary, pray that I will catch something good!"

The next morning she found a big lynx in one of her traps. A lynx pelt was worth a lot of money, money which my grandmother's sister, a widow with two children, badly needed. She told everyone that she had caught the lynx because I had prayed that she would catch something good. Everyone laughed and called out to me, "Mary, will you pray for me?"; "Mary, don't forget me in your prayers tonight!"

I stood there and hung my head. I wished the earth would open and swallow me!

I began to think that I must be growing up because sometimes in those good years, I worked in white people's homes for wages. One time in Wedgewood, I worked for the section foreman's wife. She was an English bride; she wasn't used to the lonely life in a house beside the railway tracks. She paid me to help her with her children, to wash clothes and clean her house. I remember once she wanted me to stay with her family at Wedgewood for Christmas, but my mother said, "No. Mary should come back to the village with us."

I made enough money working for this lady to order a coat from the Army and Navy store. I still remember that coat, the first new coat I ever had. It cost fourteen dollars, and it was a rust colour with fur on the cuffs. That was the first really big thing I bought for myself.

And sometimes I worked for Mrs. Silver. Like the English lady at Wedgewood, Mrs. Silver's husband worked for the railway. The family lived in a house beside the tracks in Vanderhoof, and I would leave our tent on the edge of town each day to go and clean and dust for her. I loved working for Mrs. Silver, partly because she was very kind to me, but also because her house was full of beautiful furniture which I used to shine until my face was reflected in it. I often heard her tell her friends, "Nobody can polish my stove like Mary."

One day, Mrs. Silver said to her daughter Nellie, "Go and find your brother Ken. Mary will go with you." Nellie and I walked along the tracks looking for her brother. We passed the store run by Mr. Smedley, a man with a large family. Some of his children looked out of the store window and saw Nellie and me.

They came running up beside us, yelling as they ran, "Nellie with an Indian! Nellie with an Indian!" I was sure that the whole town of Vanderhoof could hear their jeers. I wished that I could disappear. I felt sorry for Nellie—I could see that she was ashamed to be seen with a Native.

And that day I felt sorry for myself.

CHAPTER NINE

JUST AFTER MY SIXTEENTH BIRTHDAY IN 1929, I went to the home of our band chief with my parents. I did not know that this visit had anything to do with my future. I don't think I ever considered the future; the present was enough for me. I believe I thought that I would go on forever living with my parents, looking after the young ones, following the family on its seasonal wanderings. I should have known better. After all, I was now sixteen and I knew that marriages had been arranged for many girls who were my age and younger.

In our village we had watchmen. These were villagers who were appointed by the chief to arrange marriages, guard the morals of the young people, and watch over the people of the reserve. The watchmen were sometimes stern and hard. A few were different: they were appointed by the chief because they felt a concern for the welfare of the people. After 1940, we no longer had watchmen on the reserve, but when I was a girl they were powerful. Their word was law.

Walking to the chief's home, entering his house, I did not

expect my parents to tell me why we were making this visit.
I'm sure that it didn't occur to my parents to tell me that my
marriage was about to be arranged. No, just as when I first
went to school, an announcement would be made when the
plans were final. That is the way it was done in our village.

The chief and my parents talked together. I stayed in the
background, as was expected of a young girl in the presence
of her parents and the chief. I heard my parents tell the chief
that they had talked to the watchmen and that they agreed to
my marriage with Lazare John.

"When next the priest says Mass in the village, they will be
married," said the chief.

"I agree," said my mother.

Johnny nodded.

And still no one spoke to me. No one asked me, "Mary, do
you agree? Do you wish to marry this young man? Do you,
Mary, even know Lazare John?"

Now, when I remember the days before my marriage, I
think of a moth beating its wings against a lighted lamp. I
knew that there was no escape for me. The chief, my parents,
and the watchmen had decided that I was to marry Lazare
John, and from that decision there was no appeal.

I did not dream of questioning the decision or of saying to
my mother, "I don't want to get married! I want to go to
work in a hotel or a hospital or in somebody's house, a house
with nice things that I can take care of! I want a career. I don't
know anything about being married! I don't know this Lazare! I have seen him but I have never spoken to him. Please,
please, don't make me get married!" Still less did it occur to
me to say, "I won't get married! I refuse!" These things, and
many more, I said to myself day and night, but I never said
them to my mother, to the chief, or to the watchmen.

Day by day, with the arrival of the priest approaching, I
grew more scared. I knew that when I married Lazare I would
have to leave my family and live in the John home. I didn't

know anyone in his family. How could I suddenly go into the home of strangers and live as if I was one of them?

Worse still, I knew nothing about sex—what would happen to me when suddenly I was this man's wife? I had never been alone with a boy in my life. Apart from my family and relatives, I had hardly exchanged a word with someone of the opposite sex. And if my shyness had not made me avoid boys, my early training at Lejac and the knowledge that I would be the talk of the village if I was seen with a boy kept me silent. I had danced with them, but this was always under the watchful eyes of my mother and the elders.

In our culture, sex was never discussed. Most young girls were told what happened to their bodies when they became women. Young people might be warned that if they slept with an unclean person, they would get a disease. But that was all.

Lazare John was seven years older than me. I knew that he was the son of a chief, that he was considered a 'mother's boy' and that his family lived across the village from us. I had often seen him with a group of boys, but until the day we were married, I had never exchanged a word with him.

Lazare's father was Chief Vital John. His mother Margaret came from a reserve far to the south of our village. The John family, along with the Antoine family, were considered to be at the top of the social scale in the village, because both families were headed by hereditary chiefs. This gave them a good deal of status on the reserve.

Lazare was one of six children, two boys and four girls. He was the youngest son; for some reason, his mother favoured him over his older brother Felix. I had heard that when Lazare went to the Mission School in Fort St. James, his mother moved to that village to be near him. He was so unhappy away from Stoney Creek that he and his mother returned to our village after one year, and Lazare never went to school again.

Poor Lazare . . . in my distress at being ordered to marry and leave my family, it did not occur to me that he might be equally unhappy. He was no more consulted about his wishes than I was. As I was to discover, he was just as shy as his reluctant bride.

The day I dreaded arrived. The priest came to the village to say Mass. I felt as if this must be happening to someone else—it couldn't be me, Mary Paul, the girl who wanted nothing more than to live with her parents forever, who, if she left them, yearned for a career in a hospital or in a home with nice things. It couldn't be me putting on my Sunday dress and the coat I had bought so happily from the Army and Navy Store two years before. Could it be me walking to the Catholic Church in our village to be united in matrimony with a man named Lazare John? But it was.

I had gained only one small victory. A widow was going steady with my mother's first cousin, and I convinced the two of them that they should be married on the same day as me. At least there would be others in the front of the church; everyone wouldn't be looking at me.

After the ceremony, I ran home alone. I crouched in a corner of our cabin and I cried with such violence that my chest hurt. I felt as if my world had come to an end, that I had been condemned to some terrible fate that would go on forever and ever.

My parents, my relatives, came in. They tried to comfort me. Nothing helped. To me it was just like going away to school again, but now I knew that from this journey I was taking, across the village and into the house of strangers, there was no return. Finally, in an effort to cheer me, my aunt called out to me, "Why are you crying? Tonight you are going to sleep with your husband!"

I cried louder than ever.

In a few minutes, Lazare came to our cabin. He didn't look at me. He said, "Come."

And I went with him, away from my parents' home.

Looking back, I think that I was lucky. If I had to marry—and I know that given the times and our culture, there was no escape from the decision of my parents and the watchmen—I was fortunate to marry a man as kind and decent as Lazare John. Many young Native girls were not as lucky.

A day at Stoney Creek in 1982: Mary John, Sherry George, a
visiting reporter, and Margaret Nooski.

Mary and Lazare's loghouse being built on the
shore of Nulki Lake (Chapter 20).

Mary and
Lazare in
1971.

Lazare, Mary and
Helen's husband
Don at Lazare and
Mary's 50th
anniversary party
(Chapter 21).

Mary making moccasins on the steps of
her loghouse in 1985.

Mary's daughter
Helen Jones, to
whom the book
is dedicated,
in 1978.

Mary and Lazare
with four of their
grandchildren,
at a reunion at
Lelac in the
late 1970's.

Fabian John shows his grandparents Lazare and Mary the work
he's done repairing an otter skin caught by his grandmother, 1987.
(*Prince George Citizen*)

CHAPTER TEN

SO THERE I WAS, SIXTEEN YEARS OLD, married to a man who was a stranger to me. I was so ignorant, shy, afraid. All I wanted was to turn the clock back to the good old days before I knew that I would have to stand up in our little Catholic Church and find myself turned into a married woman.

It was like going away to school all over again. Now I lived only a walk of five minutes from my parents' home, just across the village, and I was as homesick as if I was one hundred miles away. I missed caring for my half brothers and sisters, I missed Johnny's loud voice and Bella's companionship, and above all, I missed my mother.

As if this wasn't bad enough, my new mother-in-law showed from the beginning that she did not think I was good enough for her son. Her attitude was confusing to me because she and her husband, like my parents, must have talked to the watchmen and agreed to the marriage. "I agree," Chief John must have said when the band chief discussed the marriage with him. Mrs. John, like my stepfather, must have nodded agreement.

But once I was in her home, it was clear to me that she did not approve of the marriage. From the first day I walked into the John cabin, I knew she felt that because of my background, I was not good enough for her son.

Looking back now, I wonder if any girl would have been good enough for Lazare in her eyes. Perhaps the most highly born princess from the richest Native band would not have suited her. I had always heard that she was possessive and that Lazare was a 'mother's boy.' I soon found out that village gossip was right. Lazare was the most important person in her life. I think that she had great ambitions for Lazare. If he had to marry, she wanted him to marry someone with Native parents.

My parentage was not the only thing about me that Mrs. John did not like. In her eyes a good Native wife learned early how to dry fish and meat, how to prepare hides, how to trap and set nets and find the places where the berries grew. She came to believe that her son was saddled with a wife who would be a burden to him and to the John family.

I realize now how useless I must have seemed to her. In Native families it was the women, as much as the men, who made certain that there was plenty of dried meat and fish and berries. Most of the meat and fish were brought home by the men, but after that, almost all of the work—the drying, the smoking, the canning—was done by women.

Native women did more than make sure that the family had a good supply of food. The families depended on wives and mothers and grandmothers to make moccasins, jackets, and mitts out of hides. To make these things, Native women had to know how to take the skins of moose and deer and scrape them and wash them and oil them. Not only did that skill mean that the family would be clothed, but also the moccasins, mitts, and jackets could be traded for clothing from white people, or sold for money.

How well a family survived often depended on the ability

of the wife to do the things that my mother and Bella, and Mrs. John herself, did so easily. I had none of the skills that a good Native wife should have had. . . .

How often my mother-in-law was mad at me in the months after the wedding! "Don't you know how to do anything?" she would ask me.

I wanted to say to her, "I wasn't trained to do these things! It was my stepsister Bella who went out with my parents, who trapped and scraped hides and dried fish. I always stayed home and looked after the kids. That was the work I learned. I was more of a baby-sitter than anything else. Please, please don't blame me!"

Of course I didn't answer back. I didn't say one word! A young bride did not talk back to her mother in law. I kept silent, but there was no happiness in my silence. Deep down, I felt that her impatience was unfair.

When we are young and unhappy, we cannot imagine that people will change, that the person who despises us today will come to love us tomorrow. And yet that is what happened in my relationship with my mother-in-law. Before she died in the 1950s, we had grown very close to each other. When she was old and needed care, I was the one who looked after her. Every day I would go to her, make up her fire in the morning, take her a cup of tea. She was thankful to have me around.

But that was many years later—in 1929 and for some years after that, neither one of us could have believed that one day she would say to me, "Lazare got himself a good wife!"

Poor Lazare! In the first few months I was submissive, but as I came to know him better, I began to demand, quietly at first, but with increasing push as the years passed, that we live in a place of our own. I was not much of a fighter, but as year followed year, I became more and more determined that we must leave our corner of the downstairs room in the John home.

It wasn't a very even struggle, which is why it lasted so

long. On the one side was a possessive mother and a son who would do anything to avoid making his mother sad. On the other side was a young girl who had never before stood up for herself, who had been trained to respect her husband and her elders and who had always done as she was told.

"When can we get our own cabin?" I would ask.

"Pretty soon," he would say.

Then I began to have babies, Winnie in 1930 when I was seventeen, Helen in 1932. And still we lived in that one room.

"Lazare," I would say, "you have to find us a place."

"Pretty soon," he would say.

I think that what finally forced him to break the ties with his mother was the fighting. In the end, when there wasn't an argument going on between his mother and me—with his mother doing most of the talking—there was an argument between me and Lazare. I was determined to get a home of my own.

The struggle to get my own place, the need for some privacy, for freedom from criticism and rejection, made me lose some of my shyness. In that struggle with Lazare and his mother, I was finally able to stand up for myself. I never became much of a fighter, but I did learn in the first four years of my marriage to wear away at my husband, like water flowing in a gentle but never-ending stream over a rock.

Finally, in 1933, Lazare could stand the bickering no longer. "Lazare," I said, "Your aunt will let us have her dead husband's shack. It is only one room, it is very small, but it will be big enough for us for the time being."

I waited for him to say "Pretty soon." He didn't. He said, "All right."

And so, after nearly five years of marriage spent in the home of my in-laws, Lazare and I and our two little girls finally had our own home.

It was so small. I was expecting again and I could see that with another baby in the shack, we would hardly be able to move in that tiny room. After a few months, I said to Lazare, "Let's start building."

I expected him to say "Pretty soon." He surprised me again. He said, "All right."

In those days, there was no help of any kind from the Department of Indian Affairs. We knew that if we wanted new housing, we were on our own. We saved a little bit of money to buy nails and other necessities, Lazare worked for some white people to get rough lumber for the floors and walls and ceiling, and we made the shakes for the roof ourselves. Within one year after we left the John home, we moved into our own two room cabin, one room downstairs, one room upstairs, furnished with a table and benches and beds that Lazare had made.

We moved in before the building was finished, but to me, finished or not, that cabin was heaven. There was room in it to move around, a place for the children to sleep upstairs, and above all, we were alone as a family. For ten years, that cabin was our home.

CHAPTER ELEVEN

LIKE MOST WOMEN, I DATE MANY of the happenings in my life from the times when my children were born. I will say, "We must have built our second house in 1943 because Bernice was just a year old when we moved into it," or, "Our ball team won that year. I remember that I was pregnant with Florence."

Over the years, between 1930, when I was seventeen, and 1949, when I was thirty-six, I had twelve children, six girls and six boys. Some were born in the village, some on the trapline or at our hunting grounds. Not one of my children was born in a hospital. My mother acted as a midwife for me; when I lost her, my aunts or other relatives were with me when I gave birth.

Some of the midwives practised the old ways of Native medicine. We call it the laying on of hands. We believe that some Native women have a gift of healing in their hands. When I was seventeen and having Winnie, my first child, there was an elderly midwife who put her hands across my back and stroked me. I can still remember how that stroking made the pain less. The labour pains did not stop, but they were greatly eased.

And oh, that cup of tea that was brought to me after each child was born tasted so good! All through the labour, a person could say to herself, "I'll have a nice cup of hot tea when this is over." There was something very comforting about the thought of that cup of tea.

One birth I remember well. Ernie, my fourth son, was born in Wedgewood in 1945. It was September, and the baby was due at any time. I thought that I would go into the hospital in Vanderhoof and deliver my baby in comfort for once. Wedgewood was only four train stops from Vanderhoof. The train came through at midnight. I thought that when my labour pains started, I would just hop on the train and for the first time in my life, enjoy the luxury of hospital care. Things didn't work out quite as I had planned.

We had two tents set up in Wedgewood with a campfire between the two. In one was Lazare, me, and our daughter Winnie who had stayed home from school to help me. In the other was Aunt Monica and her husband. He had just returned from the Second World War. My aunt and I had been working very hard, slicing up meat and scraping hides. The men had killed many moose that fall. It was heavy heavy work. Lazare intended to build a cabin so that we could spend the winter there.

Suddenly, one evening after working hard all day, my labour pains started. I dressed myself and packed a few things to take with me on the train. The pains became worse.

I said to my aunt, "I'll never be able to get on the train," and I took my clothes off. Once I was undressed, I said to Aunt Monica, "I'm afraid! What if I should start bleeding or something?"

Sick as I was, I dressed myself again—and again I realized that I would not be able to get on the train. Finally Aunt

Monica said to me, "Give up the notion of going to the hospital—you'll never make it! Have the baby here. Don't worry—we'll manage!"

The men built a big fire between the two tents, and with the light of the campfire making my tent as bright as day, Ernie was born after a long hard labour.

"It's a boy! It's a boy!" shouted Aunt Monica. "Oh, he's going to be the king of the cowboys!" Isn't it strange? To this day, Ernie would like to be a cowboy! After the birth, Aunt Monica brought me a cup of tea, and oh, it was good!

I rested in the tent for a week.

Lazare had a contract that winter to cut railway ties for a man in Prince George, and it was our intention to spend the winter in Wedgewood, where he was close to a good supply of trees. He used the week when I was resting in the tent to build a log cabin. He felled the trees, cleaned the logs, and within the week he had a good-sized cabin built, with two single windows and a lean-to at the front. He built wooden beds for the kids, and for us, a homemade table and benches. We had a good supply of food, our B.C. camp stove for heat and cooking, just like the one my parents had had in their cabin, and a coal oil lamp for light in the long winter nights.

We had a home.

In those early years, death claimed three of our children. In 1936 I gave birth to a little girl we called Shirley. Like all my older children she went to Lejac when she was six years old. How I hated sending my children off to that school!

It was terrible when the children went away. There was a loneliness in me for the whole year. A truck came each September and cleared the reserve of children. And suddenly after a summer of shouts and childish laughter, the village was silent.

Our children never came home for weekends or holidays,

not even for Christmas. They left in September and they returned in July. I could feel their homesickness at Christmas—I had experienced it myself. Lazare and I went to see them as often as we could but it was a long trip with a wagon and horses, with many stopovers on the way to Lejac and back.

I think I felt worse than Lazare when my kids left for school. He had never attended Lejac, but I had been a student there for five long years, and I knew that it had not changed. It still had whippings and porridge and hard hard work.

But what could we do? We had no choice but to send our children there. The public school in Vanderhoof would only accept Native children whose parents were enfranchised—those who had waived their rights as Native people and thus were, for example, entitled to vote. And another thing . . . with the attitude that the white people in Vanderhoof had towards Natives, we knew that, even if the school authorities accepted them, our children would be harassed by some of the white children. Lejac was terrible, but at least all the students in attendance had the same heritage, they were from the same race.

Our little Shirley—when she was seven and had been in Lejac for one year, she developed a septic throat. She was taken to St. John's Hospital in Vanderhoof, but nothing could be done for her. Maybe she should have been taken to the hospital sooner. She died there in 1943.

Another little girl, Doris, died in 1945 when she was five years old. She had tuberculosis of the stomach. We had no idea how to treat such a sickness. When her stomach became very big, we took her to the hospital in Burns Lake. It was a small hospital, with very few beds. Dr. Stone examined her and wanted to keep her in the hospital, but there were no empty beds. We could do nothing but take her home again. She died a few weeks later.

In 1947, two years after I had Ernie in Wedgewood, I gave

birth to a little boy whom we called Arthur. Shortly after his
birth, Lazare had a chance to cut mine props at Pinchi, some
miles out of Fort St. James. I took the little ones, including the
new baby, to Pinchi so that the family could be together. We
lived in a tent. The weather was terrible that year. Day after
day the rain came down, and even the stove we kept going in
the tent could not keep the dampness out. Arthur caught a
cold which developed into pneumonia. He died when he was
four months old.

———————

Like most women, I date many of the the happenings in my
life from the times when my children were born. And like
most women, I do not forget the dates when my children
were lost to me.

CHAPTER TWELVE

IN 1930, TALK OF A DEPRESSION in the white world began to filter
through to our village. In the beginning the depression meant
little to the people on our reserve. Hard times in Stoney
Creek were as natural and normal as the changing of the
seasons, the lengthening days of spring, the cold winds of
winter. We were always poor. Because there was never money
in any amount on the reserve, its lack did not affect us as it
did the white people in the areas around us. We knew that,
from the time when the first reservation was set up in Canada,
life on a reserve had always been one long depression.

Of course, as the Great Depression went on, our people
felt it. Employment for our men became scarce and finally
nonexistent. By the end of the depression the only work
available for the men was relief work. They cut side roads,
slashing down through the meadow near the village. For this
they received fifty cents a day. Many times relief money was
the only cash which was circulating on the reserve. Our hard
life became harder—that was all.

We were never without food. Every day we set our nets and brought out trout or whitefish. We'd dry or salt them, so that we would have food for the winter. Only when we needed flour or sugar or tea was the shortage of money a hardship. Almost everything else we could provide for ourselves. Lard, which was so necessary for our bannock and bread and soap-making, we could get from the fat of moose. We made our own soap, and if we could not afford a can of lye, we boiled poplar ashes, skimmed the top and had pure lye. We mixed this lye with tallow, which gave us a soft jelly-like soap that was good for cleaning.

I knew a white woman, Mrs. Campbell, a widow with small children in Vanderhoof. She and I sometimes talked about the financial situation and the hard times which people were enduring. I used to bring her a trout and in return, she would give me worn-out socks. She showed me how to take the legs of men's socks and make them into stockings for my children. Nothing in those years was wasted—nothing!

Lazare did his best to provide for our growing family. He worked for farmers at harvest time, he sold hay, cut firewood, made ties for the railway. Sometimes he would clear a piece of land for eight or ten dollars an acre. When even relief work was scarce, he hunted and trapped and fished.

My help was needed too. My mother-in-law had believed at the time of my marriage that I was going to be a burden to my husband. I knew that she was wrong and I was determined to show her that with instruction and a little patience, I could learn as quickly as the next woman. Bit by bit over the years, I mastered the skills which most Native women of my age had learned when they were girls.

With the help of my mother and my stepsister Bella, I was able to take the skin of a moose and scrape it and soak it and oil it and eventually to change it into a soft supple hide. I learned to make moccasins and jackets and mitts, and I found that, if I had one of my children or a friend with me, I could go from door to door in the white community, and say when the door was opened, "Would you like to trade a pair of moccasins (or a trout or a whitefish or a pail of berries) for some of your old clothing for my children?"

By the time I was in my mid-twenties, I had learned what I needed to know to be a good Native wife; if anything was beyond my skill, Bella and my mother were beside me, ready to help. Sometimes in the early years of my marriage, I would go to Bella in tears and say, "Look at this hide! See how stiff it is! And look at the spots on it! Oh, Lazare's mother is right! I'll never learn how to do hides!"

Bella would laugh and say, "We'll just soak this again and I'll help you to oil it more evenly. You'll see—it will turn out as nice as anything!" She was right. She would help me to do this and that and the other, and in the end I would have a soft pliable hide.

In those days, when Lazare was doing anything and everything to bring a few dollars into the home, and when I was having babies and learning the skills I would need to be a help to him, the Indian Agent was a remote figure in our lives. He had his office in Vanderhoof, and seldom drove to the reserve. When he did come to Stoney Creek, he talked to the chief and one or two of the elders. Before we knew that he was in the village, we would see the dust from his car as he hurried back to his office in town. Most of us wouldn't have recognized him if we had met him on the street.

When people on the reserve had trouble with the law or some government agency, the Indian Agent acted as their spokesman. We often laughed about the reception Natives received from the Indian Agent when they needed his help and his office was closed. No matter what the weather, the agent would keep the Native on the doorstep outside his home while he went in and bundled himself up against the weather. Then he would step outside, closing the door carefully behind him. With the wind and the snow swirling around the two of them, the problem would be discussed. I think it must have been easier to get into Buckingham Palace than into the hallway of the Indian Agent's home.

For ordinary day-to-day needs, the Indian Agent was the last person we asked for help. If people required better housing, they did what Lazare and I had done—they bought what they needed and scrounged the rest. No housing subsidies in those days!

There was no relief or welfare or family allowances for families who were raising children, nothing for widows. Anyone in need had to depend on the band or relatives or, failing that help, their own efforts. Some of the very old people received an occasional ration of food—a bit of salt, sugar, rice, lard, flour, baking powder, and tea. Apart from this help to the elderly, and one year a distribution of vegetable seeds to every family on the reserve, the Indian Agent as a source of help was as remote from us as the Prime Minister of Canada.

Because the Indian Agent had no part in our everyday lives, it has always amazed me that one time my sister-in-law Celena and I walked into Vanderhoof and went to his office to ask for help. It was during the height of the depression. Our husbands had gone out trapping, and Celena and I had given them all of our supplies—sugar, flour, tea—so that they wouldn't be out in the bush without food. When they left, the cupboards in our two cabins were bare.

We set nets and caught fish, but still, with her three children and my own three, we were desperate for flour, sugar, and salt. An idea came into our heads, God knows from where, that we would go to the Indian Agent and ask him for some supplies.

The Indian Agent at that time was an Irishman, Mr. Moore. We explained to him that our men were on the trapline, that they would be away from home for three or four weeks, we had six children and we had no food for them.

He gave us a single ration. This consisted of twenty-four pounds of flour, five pounds of rice, a bag of salt, half a pound of tea, two pounds of lard, and a bag of rolled oats. This, he said, was to do our two families for one month!

Celena and I looked at each other. Our look said, as clearly as if we had spoken, "It's going to be a long hard hungry month for the eight of us!"

As we were leaving, Mr. Moore said, "Maybe I can help you out with some clothes." He went into the back of his office and returned with some flannelette pyjamas and flannelette nightgowns, big enough for adults. He held up the nightgowns before us and he said, "Make sure you don't lift these up when your husbands come back."

Celena and I were so humiliated, we didn't know which way to look. He made us feel cheap. No man had ever talked to us like that before. Still, we clutched the flannelette nightwear to us. The material would make underclothes for our children. I believe we would have taken help from the devil himself in order to keep our children clothed!

In 1932, Lazare and I were completely without money. We talked things over with Johnny Paul and my mother and we decided that the four of us would take the boat and go trapping at Wedgewood. If we could get a few beaver, their pelts would bring a little cash into our families for clothing and basic food supplies.

We were at Wedgewood for one month. Even now I can feel the depression of those days in Wedgewood. Every day we followed the trapline only to find trap after trap empty. In that time, we managed to trap four muskrats. Their pelts sold for twenty-five cents each, which gave us earnings of one dollar for one month of setting traps and tramping through the bush.

At the end of the month, we decided to return to Stoney Creek; we could see that the animals had deserted our trapline and that there was no money to be made at Wedgewood that spring. I will never forget the trip back, up the Nechako River to Vanderhoof.

Johnny and Lazare had to pole the boat, laden with our supplies, upstream all the way. In order to lighten the load, my mother and I walked. This was in the spring of the year. It was still chilly and the clothing we wore was light. We felt sorry for ourselves, but when we thought of Johnny and Lazare struggling against the river current, we knew that we didn't have the worst of the trip.

Fortunately, when we arrived in Vanderhoof, we found an old fellow with a truck. We loaded everything from the boat into the truck and finally we arrived back at Stoney Creek, weary, footsore, and broke. We had one dollar to show for one month's work, the hardships of the trapline and the trip back up the Nechako River.

The next year, 1933, we were luckier. We trapped several beaver, and at the end of the month, we had cleared fifty-four dollars. After the disaster of the year before, that fifty-four dollars was a fortune to us. We laid in a good supply of flour and sugar and tea and we said to ourselves, "Good! Now we'll survive the winter!"

Remembering the hardships of those years, it is easy to forget that there were good times too. There was much visiting, sometimes whole days when we would sit around kitchen tables and chat and drink tea. We had to make our own social life. The men were usually away working or in the bush hunting, and the women were left with small children. Trips to town were rare. We had no transportation and no money. Visiting was our substitute for radios and television sets and shopping trips.

Lazare was a great sportsman. He was one of the driving forces in organizing a hockey team, and was himself one of the stars of our Stoney Creek team. The wives of the hockey players were kept busy making and mending uniforms for the team. The uniforms, I remember, were red, white, and blue, with stars sewn here and there. We knitted their mitts, sweaters, caps, socks, and we made the leggings out of canvas.

Baseball was popular at the time. Stoney Creek had a very strong team which used to play the other reserves, as well as many of the towns within driving distance. Again, Lazare was active in the baseball league and played on the team.

My friend Veronica George and I often talk about the time in 1933 when we went with the baseball team to a tournament in Prince George. We set up our tents in the Island Cache, and while the men played ball, Veronica and I went from door to door in Prince George, trading moccasins for second-hand clothes. We came home with a big stock of very good used clothing.

"Look at this and this and this!" I said to Veronica, holding up skirts and trousers and jackets.

"The people of Prince George must be very rich people to give away such good clothing," said Veronica. I agreed. We had enough clothing to keep us supplied for a year or more. And best of all, the Stoney Creek ball team skunked the Prince George team on that trip!

The Stoney Creek ball team travelled all over in those depression years: Quesnel, Wells, the reserves at Fort St. James and Fraser Lake and Burns Lake. They would tumble into Lazare's father's car, a Model T, and ride off in high spirits, ready to play for the honour of Stoney Creek.

Oh, we were proud of our hockey team, our ball team! Every victory was a victory for the whole village, every defeat convinced us that the weather or the umpire or the playing field was at fault. Win or lose, our men could do no wrong.

And what dances we had in those years! We had no hall. Somebody would say, "I'll have a dance in my house tonight!" Out would come all the furniture—beds, tables, benches —clearing the floor for a great old time. In the morning, everyone would gather and move the furniture back into the cabin. Lazare played the drums, his brother-in-law played the violin, and Albert Williams was on the banjo. Many times before a dance these three would gather in the upstairs room of our house and practise, hour after hour, to get a tune just right.

The children and I enjoyed these musical sessions. We didn't mind the noise one bit. We liked it.

CHAPTER THIRTEEN

1934 WAS A YEAR I WILL NEVER FORGET. The year started with both my mother and me expecting children. My mother was thirty-four, and although she had had several pregnancies, she had only three living children, apart from me. Mark in that year was fourteen, Alec was seven, and the youngest, Melanie, was five years old. In 1934, I was twenty-one years old and expecting my fourth child.

So there we were, mother and daughter, both of us young, both of us in the family way.

Johnny Paul, my stepfather, was forty-three years old that year. He was still the sociable, loud, happy-go-lucky man who had taken me into his home as a child of five and had treated me, from the beginning, as his own flesh and blood.

Johnny was renowned in Stoney Creek as a hunter, a trapper, a provider. He was also known in the village as a man who enjoyed a drink. He was not a steady drinker, but we always knew that when he went into Prince George, he would return with a bottle of rum or whiskey bought from a bootlegger or in the local liquor store for him by one of his white friends.

In those days, Natives were not allowed to go into beer parlors. They could not buy liquor at a liquor store, or have alcohol on the reserve. Sometimes people made homebrew, but unless my memory of those years is wrong, there was very little alcohol abuse in our village. The two or three people in Stoney Creek who drank to excess stood out like lights—the villagers did not approve of them, and the chief made life as miserable for them as he could.

In January, 1934, Johnny went with a friend of his, James Antoine, to visit Johnny's brother Gus. Gus lived down at the other end of the lake and it was known that he sometimes made home-brew. When Johnny and his friend James returned to the village, they were very sick and in great pain. Day by day, their health got worse. Within one month, both men were dead. Their deaths were talked about only in whispers, for the making and drinking of homebrew was illegal.

My mother did not discuss the cause of Johnny's death with me or with anyone, but from the little bits I heard here and there, I learned that Gus had made homebrew in a coal oil can. The can had not been washed to cleanse it of its deadly liquid. Johnny and James must have drank coal oil along with the home brew.

When the two men were dead, one of my friends whispered to me, "That coal oil ate their insides clear away."

I thought, when my mother lost Johnny, that nothing worse could happen to her. There she was, a thirty-four-year-old widow, pregnant, and with three young children to support. There was no help from the government or the Department of Indian Affairs, no widow's allowance, no welfare, nothing.

Little did I know that there was worse to come. A few weeks after Johnny's death, my mother went out to help fourteen-year-old Mark put a hay rack on the sleigh. Mark was going out to the meadow to get a load of feed for the horses. The hay rack was too heavy for Mark to lift alone; my mother was strong, and had never spared herself when it came to heavy work. She helped him to lift the rack on to the sleigh.

Within a few hours, she began to hemorrhage. For one month the blood kept coming. She tried to keep up with her usual work, but we could see that she was becoming weaker each day.

My Grandmother Ann, my Aunt Monica, and I were with her on the twenty-eighth of April when her labour started. Within a short time, her dead baby was born, and in a few hours, my mother was dead too.

Her last hours on earth were not peaceful. Johnny's sister was at her bedside. This sister did not know what had caused her brother's death; she was half crazy with grief at the loss of her brother and seemed to blame my mother for not telling her why Johnny had died. My grandmother and aunt and I could only stand by helplessly as this woman said terrible things to my mother. Once, I remember, she screamed at her, "You say you're sick! If we're sick we die!"

My mother turned her face to the wall, tears streaming down her cheeks. She spoke once. "I only wish she knew what her brother died of," she said. And then my mother died.

By the time my son Ray was born, it was all over. The cabin where Johnny and my mother had lived with their children stood empty. That empty cabin meant the destruction of a family. Where once my young mother had moved silently, where Johnny had shouted and laughed until the walls seemed to echo with his high spirits, where Mark and Alec and Melanie had played their childish games and told their little stories in their own home—all, all, was silent.

The church bell tolled. The village grieved.

My own grief . . . there are still no words to describe what the loss of my mother meant to me.

CHAPTER FOURTEEN

LIFE GOES ON. WHEN, IN THE MIDDLE of a depression a woman has a husband and a growing family, when the struggle to survive, to keep food on the table and the family clothed, takes all of her energy, there is no time to grieve, to look back with sorrow and regret. Mark and Alec and Melanie had no parents—we had to think of the living and try, if we could, to forget the fresh graves in the village cemetery.

By this time, my stepsister Bella was married to Mike Ketlo. Once my mother's funeral was over and the shock of her death had lifted a little, Bella and her husband, Lazare and I, sat together and discussed the future of the three children. In the end it was decided that Bella would take Melanie and that Mark and Alec would live with me. Eventually, Melanie and Alec went to Lejac; Mark stayed with Lazare and me until he died.

A white friend of mine told me about an old song that has the line: "Consumption has no pity for blue eyes and golden hair." I guess it doesn't have pity for the dark eyes and hair of the Native people either.

Mark, my half-brother, was five years younger than me. He was twenty-two years old in 1940, when the Second World War was going on. He was called to Vancouver to undergo a medical for getting into the army. Before he left Stoney Creek, he could talk of nothing but what he would do and where he would go when he was a soldier. He did not pass his medical. It was discovered that he had tuberculosis. He grew depressed when he couldn't get in the army and instead of going into a hospital for treatment or coming home to me, he wandered the streets of Vancouver, sleeping out at night, bumming around during the day.

Finally, when he was almost dead, he was taken to the tuberculosis sanitorium at Coqualeetza near Hope in British Columbia. I was notified that he was there.

I was determined that Mark would not die away from his family. I did everything but beg, borrow and steal until I had my return fare so that I could visit him. When I finally reached him, I could see that he had not long to live. He begged me to take him out of the hospital, to bring him home with me. I went to the doctors.

"I want to take my brother back to Stoney Creek," I said.

"We cannot agree to that," they answered. "We do not believe he will survive such a trip."

"He is going to die, whether it is here or there," I replied. "He wants to die in his own village."

The doctors argued, but their words meant nothing to me. I remembered myself as a little girl, in bed sick with the 1918 flu, and an old woman coming to me and saying, "You have a baby brother. His name is Mark." This was the brother whom I had looked after as an infant and a little boy, and who had come into my home and my care after my mother's death . . . no, I would not leave him to die alone in a strange building.

The doctors finally threw up their hands. Mark came home with me. I will never forget the trip back to Stoney Creek. Mark was put in a berth; I had a lower berth beside him. I lifted him and turned him—he was as light as a feather, just skin and bones. More than once, I thought he would die before I could get him back to our village.

My aunt and I put him in my parents' old house, and there we looked after him until he died. How he fought for his life! He was determined to live.

"Mary," he said to me over and over, "I don't want to die! I'm only twenty-two years old!"

He lived just one week after I brought him back to Stoney Creek. But at least he died in his village, surrounded by his own people.

We knew so little about tuberculosis. We didn't know that it was infectious, that extra precautions had to be taken to prevent the spread of this dread disease.

We took in a young boy, an orphan, who had tuberculosis. Many village people told us that it was dangerous to have him in our home, but we ignored their warnings. Lazare and I thought it was a matter of simple charity to offer the dying boy a home. The Indian Agent gave him a small ration each month, but apart from that, nobody in the Indian Agent's office or in the public health showed an interest in the welfare of the boy or warned us of the dangers to which we were exposing our own children.

The poor young boy took a long time to die. We gave him what care and comfort we could, but in the end, he had no resistance with which to fight the disease.

Not long after he died, in 1952, we discovered that our two little sons, Ernie and Gordie, had tuberculosis. Fortunately, they were not badly infected, but nevertheless, they were hospitalized in Miller Bay Hospital near Prince Rupert. They were away from me for a year, and in that time, I was only able to pay them one visit. When I saw them, they were in the same crib, fighting and rough-housing and as lively as they could be.

The nurses loved them. "They are real little imps," said one nurse to me. On that visit, Gordie and Ernie showed very little interest in me; as the youngest and most lively patients in the hospital, they were surrounded with love and attention. Because they were so young, they had become used to the hospital quickly.

I still remember how lonely I felt as I left them, tumbling over each other in their crib. I was relieved that they were not homesick, but how empty my house in Stoney Creek seemed when I returned after that visit to Miller Bay!

I believe it was my daughter Helen and her battle with tuberculosis which nearly broke my heart. She was my second child, born in 1932, and in a way that I cannot put into words, we were so close that sometimes each of us seemed part of one whole. When things went badly for Helen, it was as if they were happening to me.

When she was of age to attend school, Helen was taken to Lejac; I suffered homesickness and hunger and anxiety with her, almost as if I was reliving my own years in that institution. She left school when she was fourteen and found work on the cleaning staff in Miller Bay Hospital. Within a year, she was a patient in the hospital where she had been working.

She was hospitalized for fifteen years. Her entire girlhood was spent as a patient in Miller Bay and then in Coqualeetza, near Hope, where poor Mark had spent such a short time.

Helen cried a lot when she was in Miller Bay. She would write to us, begging us to come and see her, or to send her crochet cotton or knitting wool so that she would have activities that would keep her busy. How bitter it was for Lazare and me that we could visit her only once in a while! How I hated our poverty when I had to write to her and say that we could not afford to send her even a ball of wool. Those were hard hard years for Helen and our family.

When she had been in Miller Bay for some years, she met a man from Skidegate Indian Reserve on the Queen Charlottes. He was called Swede Jones. After many years, when she was discharged from the hospital as cured, she and Swede were married in the United Church in Skidegate. No doubt she would have been married in our little Catholic Church in Stoney Creek, if her sister Winnie had not had an unfortunate experience with our priest.

Winnie had also met a Haida from Skidegate, Ed Young, whom she wished to marry. Ed was a member of the United Church. Winnie brought Ed to her father and me and told us that they wished to be married. Lazare and I went to the priest in Stoney Creek, a Frenchman.

"Our daughter Winnie wishes to marry Ed Young, who is a Protestant," we said to the priest. "Will you marry them in our village church?"

"No," said the priest. "I cannot marry a Protestant in our church. Your daughter should marry a good Catholic boy."

Lazare and I were insistent. "She does not want to marry a Catholic boy. She wants to marry this Ed Young!"

"You and your husband are committing a sin when you encourage this marriage," said the priest. "You will be sorry if you continue with this foolishness!"

Lazare and I, Winnie and Ed, returned to our home. We talked things over. Lazare and I had given our consent to this marriage, and we were not willing to withdraw it. In the end, we journeyed to Prince George and Winnie and Ed were married in the home of the United Church minister. The following Sunday at Mass, all hell broke loose!

The priest announced from the pulpit that because Mary and Lazare John had consented to their daughter's marriage outside the church, they and their whole family were excommunicated. Well! Everybody in the village was furious.

"It's not up to him to excommunicate any person!" said one.

"Only the bishop has the right to excommunicate!" said another.

"Just ignore him!" said a third.

And that's just what Lazare and I did! We went to Mass the next Sunday as usual. We went to Confession, we took Communion, and never once, not on that Sunday or on any other Sunday, did the priest refuse us the sacraments of the church. His excommunication just faded away.

He was a strange man, a good man and yet, a kind of dictator too. I remember that he was very upset with Gus, Johnny Paul's brother. After Johnny's death, Gus left his wife, enfranchised himself and set up housekeeping with a white woman. The priest was bothered about Gus, and said more than once, "If Gus were to die, I wouldn't know what to do with him." Gus had many friends on the reserve and this kind of talk from the priest angered people.

"What do you mean?" they asked. "Gus is Catholic. Why wouldn't he be buried like any other Catholic?"

"No," said the priest, "I wouldn't know what to do about him. I couldn't have a service for him in our church, and I wouldn't want to have him buried in our cemetery." There was much grumbling in the village about the priest, about his efforts to excommunicate Lazare and me, and his statements about Gus.

And yet, when Lazare and I were building our second house, the one we lived in until just a few years ago, this French priest came over many times and helped us put up walls and work on the roof. He never once apologized for trying to drive us out of the church.

And poor Helen . . . her troubles were not over. Before long her tuberculosis flared up again and she was back in

Miller Bay. Finally, in a last desperate effort to save her, she was removed to the sanitorium in Coqualeetza, and one lung was removed. She was nearly thirty before she was finally out of the sanitorium. By that time, she and Swede were separated. The marriage was at an end.

Helen worked on the Queen Charlottes, and, in later years with Stoney Creek students attending St. Joseph's School in Vanderhoof. For seven years, she was the band manager on the reserve. Time and again, she found herself back in hospital. At those times we knew that her one over-worked lung was unable to do the work that needed two.

A few months ago, we lost her.

As if tuberculosis had not robbed me of enough, there was another sorrow for me. When she was in her mid-forties, Bella, who had been a sister and more than a sister to me, died of tuberculosis in her home in Stoney Creek. I was with her when she died.

CHAPTER FIFTEEN

THE PEOPLE OF STONEY CREEK had never stopped pushing the Catholic Church and the Department of Indian Affairs to set up a day school on the reserve. We felt that it was too hard, for parents as well as the children, to send the boys and girls off to Lejac in September each year, and to see nothing of them until July of the next year. We hardly knew our children when they came home in the summer. Brothers and sisters were separated in the school. Our people knew that the residential school system was destroying Native family life. Our culture and our language would have vanished from the village without the elders keeping them alive.

Finally, in 1951, the villagers had their wish. A day school was set up on the reserve. From the beginning, we had nothing but trouble with the school.

The major problem was with the teachers. The Department of Indian Affairs would never pay the teachers what they would have received if they had worked in the public school system. The result was that almost always, our children received instruction from poorly qualified teachers who had trouble finding jobs in the white community. More than this, many of the teachers had had no previous contact with Natives. Suddenly, they were expected to live on a reserve, with its lack of modern facilities, its isolation from the kind of life and companionship familiar to them, and a culture which often seemed strange to them.

Oh, it was one crisis after another!

One poor soul I remember well. She had come from the United States, a middle-aged woman with two children. She must have watched every Hollywood movie ever made which showed Indians scalping and burning and raping. She did not understand our people, and because she did not understand us, she was afraid. Her solution to her problems was to drink.

I remember talking to a social worker from the provincial Department of Welfare, Bridget Moran, about this teacher. She told me that the Indian Agent, a man named Mr. Howe, asked her to visit the teacher and investigate charges being made about the operation of the day school. The children of Stoney Creek, he said, were complaining to their parents about the names the teacher called them, and the abuse she heaped on them as potential scalpers, rapists, and cannibals.

"I called in at the teacherage after school hours," Bridget told me. "It was winter and was already dusk when I knocked on the teacherage door. I found the teacher crouched in the dark, with doors and windows barricaded. The poor soul believed that she was in an ambush and was expecting a raid at any moment. She could visualize herself and her two children with scalps missing. She was convinced that there was a lineup of males, men and boys, outside her door, patiently waiting their turn in order to enter her house and rape her. From what she said, I gathered that she and her children spent every night in the dark. She seemed to feel that a light in her teacherage would be the signal for an attack!"

I spent many nights with this woman, trying to calm her

fears, and, if I am honest, also doing my best to keep her from drinking. In the end, she returned to United States. When I last heard of her, she was receiving treatment in a psychiatric hospital in Washington State.

This woman was an extreme example of the kind of teacher employed in our day school; others came and went, leaving little to remind us that they had once spent some time in our village.

Finally, the Catholic Church, the Department of Indian Affairs, and the Chief and Band Council decided to set up a school in Vanderhoof, and to bus the children from Stoney Creek into Vanderhoof each day. St. Joseph's School came into being. It solved some, if not all, of the problems of our children's education.

We seemed to overcome one problem only to be faced with another. Until 1957, our men could always count on making money cutting ties for the railway. This was piece work, and was seasonal, but until 1957, it brought needed cash into the village. In 1957, the railway companies decided to use a different type of wood and to treat ties in processing plants. Suddenly, there was no money to be made from the railway.

Lazare and I were desperate. We had bought an old truck and were making payments of fifty-six dollars each month for it. We now had our children with us for twelve months of every year, which was our wish, but where was the money for food and clothing to come from? We sat at our homemade table and added and subtracted, but no matter how many scraps of paper we filled with figures, there was still no money to meet our expenses.

Finally, in desperation, I went to Sister Superior in St. John's Hospital in Vanderhoof.

"I wonder," I said, "if you would give me a job cleaning or in the laundry?"

"Don't you have children at home?"

"Yes," I said, "I have six of my children at home."

"How old is the youngest?"

"That's Gordie," I answered. "He's nine years old."

She looked at me for a few minutes. Then she said, "You have a family at home and you should look after them. I think your place is in the home."

I said, "We're desperate. Somebody has to go to work. My husband can't work, because the kind of work he was doing isn't done any more."

She seemed to think for a long time. Finally she said, "I will put your name down. If we need you, we'll call you."

A week went by. One cold windy morning in April, a taxi drew up to our door.

"You are to go to the hospital tomorrow morning for work," said the taxi driver.

Early the next morning—I remember there was a cold north wind blowing—I got up early and hiked over the creek to Mike Ketlo's house. From there I phoned a taxi to pick me up for work. The taxi cost me five dollars, which was just about what I made for my first day's work at the hospital. Little did I know then that I would work in the hospital for thirteen years.

This was my first real venture into the white world. I had worked for white people like Mrs. Silver before I was married, and I had knocked on many doors in the white community, trading fish or moccasins for used clothing, but at those times, I was always Mary the Indian. Suddenly, I found myself working side by side with white people. I was expected to talk to them, to laugh with them, to eat and drink tea with them.

No! It was impossible! I was so shy that I wouldn't go into the tea room when we had our breaks. I would take my tea and sandwich and sit outside, or slip into the laundry room. I couldn't eat in front of white people. I would hide my food. I was ashamed even to drink tea in the same room with them—I felt as if they would hear the tea as it went down into my stomach!

More than one person befriended me. A German woman, who did not speak very good English, coaxed me to come into the tearoom with her. "Come on," she would say. "Nobody bite you!"

Another woman, Mrs. Morrison, who worked in the laundry, often asked me to join her on our coffee breaks. "Come along, Mary," she would say to me. "I'll sit with you. I promise that I won't leave you."

It took a very long time before I was able to go into that room, with white people all around me, and eat my sandwich and drink my tea with any feeling of ease.

My routine was the same each day. I cleaned the first floor of the hospital, and when that was finished, I went into the laundry in the basement and ironed and folded clothes. Twenty minutes before quitting time, I went back upstairs and ran over the hall floor with a dust mop. By that time, I had worked my eight hours.

———————

Since Stoney Creek was nine miles from Vanderhoof and there was no bus service, getting back and forth to work was a problem for me. Sometimes our old truck made the trip, sometimes I hitchhiked, sometimes I walked.

One day in February, when I had been working in the hospital for a few months, Lazare said to me, "I don't know how you'll get to work tomorrow. I can't get the truck to start."

Now, here was a problem! I had never been late for work, no matter what problems I had getting there, and that night, I promised myself that I would arrive at work on time the next morning.

I didn't sleep that night. At three o'clock in the morning, my son Ernie (who was about twelve years old at the time) and I climbed out of bed and prepared for the long walk into town. The road was a sheet of ice—there had been a thaw earlier followed by a deep frost. I put heavy men's socks over my boots and Ernie and I started out. We walked on glare ice for four hours.

I arrived at work a few minutes before I was to start cleaning the first floor. I was just about dead, I was so tired. I was in a panic. "I don't think I will be able to work," I said to myself.

Mrs. Morrison looked at me. "Mary," she said, "whatever is the matter?"

I told her that my young son and I had been walking since three o'clock in the morning on glare ice to make sure that I got to work on time.

"None of that now," she said to me. "You go into the night watchman's room and sleep there for a few hours. Mrs. Adams and I will manage without you." And oh, did that cot in the night watchman's room feel good when I finally stretched out.

I knew that between the struggle to get back and forth to the hospital and the work I had to do when I arrived home after my eight hours of employment, I wasn't going to be able to go on. I had six children attending school. I had to wash clothes, bake bread and buns—one night, I remember I baked seventy-two buns!—make supper, clean the house, all after a hard day's work. We were still living in our little cabin. I had none of the modern conveniences such as running water or an electric stove. Everything was done the hard way. The kids were as helpful as they could be, but it was still too big a load for one woman.

I tried one thing after another. For a while, I rented a small house in Vanderhoof. My pay was $125 each month. When I had paid the rent, power, lights, and sewer for the house I had less than $100 left to feed and clothe myself and our six children. The house was small, but I thought I was in heaven when I turned on taps and out came hot and cold water!

During that time, in order to bring in a little extra money, I found a job on my day off. I cleaned house for the hospital bookkeeper and his wife, a woman who worked in medical records. How good they were to me! I felt at home with them; never once did this couple give me the feeling that I was lower than they were.

A friend of mine, Margaret Antoine, was working at the hospital. We were both paying rent and having a hard time stretching our pay to cover our expenses. We talked things over.

"The weather is getting nice," said Margaret.

"Yes," I said. "If we had tents, we could live in them for the summer and save the money we are paying out in rent."

No sooner said than done! I bought a big tent. Lazare put down flooring and built walls about three feet high and I set up my tent. Margaret set her tent up beside me. We used to laugh that we still had running water— we were on the edge of a creek. The walk back and forth to the hospital was about three miles, but at least we were not paying out money for rent.

We were tough in those days! We had a stove inside the tent for cooking and warmth, and as long as the weather stayed warm and dry, we enjoyed living out of doors. Eventually, Margaret Antoine's sister Virgie set up her tent beside us. A little later we were joined by my sister-in-law Celena. We were like a little Native village, there on the edge of Vanderhoof.

We had only one problem—one of the doctors was worried that we were using the creek water for drinking and cooking.

"I'll let all of you stay where you are," he said, "as long as you get your drinking water from the town water supply or a proper well."

The closest well, with an outside pump, was at Mrs. Silver's home. This was about a mile from our camp. The kids hauled our water for drinking and cooking each day, and for the rest, washing and cleaning, we still had our running water in the creek!

The early years when I worked at the hospital were hard on Lazare and hard on our marriage.

Native women of my generation had always worked hard, but that work was done within the family and in traditional ways. It was a blow to Lazare's pride that I was supporting the family while he was idle. His friends made remarks which hurt him—"Did you get your old lady off to work to-day?"—and this hurt was brought into our marital relationship. I did not blame him because he was unemployed. He had always been a hard worker and a good provider, and it was only force of circumstance which forced me to work out of the home. But when a man's pride is injured, it takes more than his wife's soothing words to heal the wounds.

It was a lucky break that the powerline was being put through in 1959. Lazare, along with many village men, found employment that summer. The work was only seasonal and finished in the fall, but at least he could feel that he was doing his part in supporting the family. The next year, 1960, he was given a part-time job at St. Joseph's School, which paid him $100 each month.

The following year, we hit the jackpot! Lazare put in an application for a steady job as a labourer with the Department of Highways. He was lucky enough to get hired on, and worked until he was sixty-six years old, at which time he had to retire.

Now, things were easier, easier between Lazare and me, easier financially too. We saved a little money here, a little money there, and were finally able to invest in a good vehicle. My children and I could move back to Stoney Creek where we had always wanted to be. Now we had a truck which was reliable. Lazare and I were both on the day shift. We drove to work together. He would drop me at the hospital, drive on to the highway department's yard, leave the truck there and go to the section of roadway where he was assigned to work.

There was no more hitchhiking to work, no more walking on glare ice in the middle of the night in order to get to work on time. What a change!

———————

One day in 1972, when I had been working at the hospital for thirteen years, Father Dalton came to me.

"Mary," he said, "we would like you to come and work at St. Joseph's School."

I was stunned. "Father," I said, "what can I do in the school? I am no teacher!"

"We want you to teach the children their native language. If we don't do this soon, the Carrier language will be lost to the new generation."

How strange! I thought. The church took away our language and now they are trying to give it back to us.

"We will give you the same pay as you are now getting at the hospital," he said, "and you will work fewer hours. Will you think about it? I will wait for your answer."

I promised to think it over. To be honest, for the next few days I couldn't think of anything else. I was torn in two directions. On the one hand, I was happy with my job in the hospital. I had become used to working with the white community, and I had very close friends on the hospital staff. On the other hand, I knew that what Father Dalton said was the truth. The new generation were the children of Natives who had attended Lejac Residential School, and who had been whipped every time they spoke their own language. Most of the parents of the students in St. Joseph's School had lost their language. If someone didn't teach it to the children growing up, the Carrier language would be lost forever.

I had really very little choice. I gave two weeks notice to

the hospital. I still have the gift the staff gave me at my going-away party.

—————————

Many times in my life I have wondered why the church and the government got together years ago and almost destroyed our culture. I guess they thought they had to do that to convert the Native peple, the savages, as they called us. They thought that we had no God, that we didn't know God. But a long time ago my people knew that there was a Great Spirit, a Being. In the late 1960s or the early 1970s, the church and the government must have realized their mistake, and I was caught right up in the middle of that. Maybe they were forced into giving our language and our culture back to us. Maybe the new leaders, the young people, put pressure on them. Whatever the reason, the Catholic school must have thought I was the right person for the job.

I didn't have any teacher's training, but I worked with the young people as best I could. I taught music and dancing, as well as the Carrier language. I knew our language, but I had to depend on Lazare for the songs and dances. He taught them to me and then I taught them to the students of St. Joseph's School. It wasn't easy—so little in our culture is written down.

So there I was, Mary John, formerly a student in Lejac, now a teacher of the Carrier language and songs and dances in a Catholic school. Isn't life strange?

Mary and Briget Moran at the launch for *Stoney Creek Woman* at Mosquito Books in Prince George, 1988.

Mary being presented with the Order of Canada by Governor-General Roméo LeBlanc in April 1997.

Lazare in front of the Potlatch House at Stoney Creek in 1991.

Mary and Lazare at their 60th anniversary party
in 1989.

Lazare's funeral in 1996.

Mary and her granddaughter Melanie in 1996.

Bridget, receiving an
Honorary Doctor of
Law degree from the
University of Northern
British Columbia, with
Mary in 1995.

Mary John in Victoria, 1997.

CHAPTER SIXTEEN

SO MUCH OF OUR LIVES WAS RUN by the Indian Act. I wasn't very old before I knew that under this Act, Natives were forbidden to buy or drink liquor or to have alcohol on their reservations. Often there was talk about this restriction in our village, especially when the Mounties picked up one of the villagers who had been drinking. As small children we listened to this talk and it came to us early in our lives that we were different, that laws were made for us which white people did not have to obey.

As a child, I had seen Johnny Paul bring a bottle of whiskey into our house after a trip to Prince George and I had heard him describe how Scotty or Barney or some other white man had bought the bottle for him at the local liquor store. Johnny sometimes spoke of this or that white man who had spent time in jail because he had bought a bottle of rum or whiskey for a Stoney Creek villager.

The big change came after the Second World War. So many men from Stoney Creek and reserves all across Canada had served overseas in the armed forces, in England, Scotland, France, Italy, and Germany. They drank in canteens, as they called the beer parlors, just like white soldiers. When those who survived the war returned to Canada, the Native ex-servicemen found that under the Indian Act they were still forbidden to drink alcohol anywhere in their own country.

People say that it was the returned soldiers who brought about a change in the Indian Act in 1952. That change said that Natives could drink off the reserve. This meant that we could go into pubs, beer parlors, and cocktail lounges and drink as much as we wanted. We still could not bring liquor to the reserves or into our own homes. How often I watched the results of this policy! People would drink as much as they could before closing time, because they knew that once they left the beer parlor, the only place they could drink was in some back alley or beside the railway tracks.

In 1961 we were allowed to vote on whether or not liquor could be brought to the reserve. Like most reserves, Stoney Creek voted to allow liquor in our village. I heard that some of the reserves in the north didn't hear about the vote and lost the chance to drink in their homes.

Even after 1961, it wasn't clear sailing for a Native who wanted to have a drink. Under the Government Liquor Act, a magistrate could make it illegal for a person to drink. When that happened, his name was placed on what was called an Interdict List. More than one person from our village was on that list and if he drank, he went to jail and with him, the person who had supplied him with liquor.

Someone told me that in 1965 or 1966, a group of Prince George lawyers, Don Kennedy and others, checked the number of people who had served time in jail in Prince George because they had violated the Interdict List. Of the 173 names given to the lawyers, one man was white—the rest were Natives. When this information was sent to Victoria, the Interdict List was repealed for Northern British Columbia.

Long afterwards I heard that in the early 1950s, the magistrate in Burns Lake, about 100 miles west of us, put every resident on the Burns Lake Reserve on the Interdict List, even those under the legal drinking age, despite the fact that it was legal for Natives to drink.

Alcohol and Magistrates and the Indian Act—what a book that would make!

Before 1952, when we visited Vanderhoof, unless the weather was warm and we could build our campfire among the willows, the visit didn't last very long. After all, there was little enjoyment in walking the streets hour after hour on a cold November day, looking in at the windows of cafés and beer parlors that we were forbidden to enter. We used to say that the only time we could socialize in Vanderhoof with any pleasure was when we were admitted to what was called the Indian Wing of St. John's Hospital. Then, if we weren't too sick, we could have a good gossip in comfort.

The reaction of Stoney Creek villagers when finally we could go into beer parlors and cocktail lounges was, "Now we're as good as white people!"

I thought that myself. It was a startling change. One day we were forbidden to drink, and the next day we were welcome in the Vanderhoof Hotel. Suddenly, there was a place in Vanderhoof where we could meet our friends in a warm comfortable environment and visit—and drink—to our hearts' content.

I had never cared about alcohol, but in 1952, I was just like everybody else. How nice it was on a Friday afternoon when the week's work was done, to meet Sophie Thomas and Veronica George, have a few drinks and a good gossip! How nice it was to meet my husband and his friends and sit in a friendly atmosphere and drink and exchange the latest news! We drank when we went to dances. A friend and I would buy a bottle on a weekend and say to each other, "Now we are going to have a high old time!"

Yes, I was like everyone else. I didn't drink to excess, except on one occasion, but alcohol became a part of my social life. On that one occasion when I did drink too much, Lazare wouldn't stop drinking, and I thought I would join him instead of fighting with him. I found out then that excessive drinking did not agree with me, and like many other people I vowed to myself, "Never again!"

In 1957, everything changed. Early one morning, just as dawn was breaking, there was a knock at my door. When I answered, I found two Mounties standing on the step. They told me that a young couple, the parents of three children, had been killed in a train accident. The man was my husband's nephew. The Mounties said that the young couple were on the railway tracks when a train backed out of a siding.

I dressed as fast as I could and ran over to the house of this young couple. There were the three little children, sound asleep, unaware that they had lost their parents.

I was in shock. All day I walked the floor, thinking of the young couple. I knew that they had been drinking heavily, hanging around the back alleys of Vanderhoof and down near the station.

Finally, the next day, I forced myself to go and see the bodies. I have never forgotten the sight that met my eyes in the morgue of St. John's Hospital.

The young man had lost both legs at the thighs, and his guts were hanging out. People told me they found bits and pieces of him all along the tracks, enough to fill a shoe box. His wife was not as badly injured as her husband. She was wearing a pink dress which looked as if it had been caught in the engine. She must have been dragged for some distance.

To this day, I remember the pink dress that young mother was wearing when she was killed.

For days I asked myself over and over again, "Why? Why?" And something inside me answered, "Alcohol!" At that moment I made a vow that I would never touch alcohol again.

So that other people would understand and accept that I no longer took a drink, I went to Father Dalton and in his presence I took a life pledge. He gave me a medal. I had hoped that other villagers would do the same, including some members of my own family, but I was the only one to make this solemn vow. I have never had a drink since that day in 1957 when I stood before Father Dalton and took the pledge. At banquets, I turn my glass upside down; at parties, I make myself a big pot of tea or sip a glass of water.

And always I hope that my abstinence will be an example to other Natives, especially to the young people.

CHAPTER SEVENTEEN

IN 1942, SOMETHING NEW CAME into the lives of Stoney Creek
women. A white woman, a teacher named Mrs. Murphy,
came to us and told us about a new organization, started by
the Department of Indian Affairs in Ottawa, which was
spreading to the reservations across Canada.

"It is called the Homemakers," Mrs. Murphy said. "You set
yourselves up with a president and vice-president and secretary, like the service clubs in Vanderhoof and Prince George.
You should apply for funding to the Indian Agent in order to
get started."

"And what does this club do?" we asked.

"It brings Native women together to do handicrafts, to
exchange ideas on child care and ways in which home life can
be improved. You meet once a week or once a month or
whatever, and you make quilts and you knit. On other reserves, the Native women hold bazaars where they sell their
handicrafts and make money to buy more yarn or material, or
they use the money to buy something for the reserve. Some-

times, on these other reserves, speakers such as public health nurses or social workers are invited to talk to the Homemakers. There are conferences in Vancouver, and once a year, Homemakers from across Canada meet in Duck Lake, Aberta and talk about ways to improve family life for Natives. If you get organized, one of your members would go to those conferences."

The women of my village met and discussed the information Mrs. Murphy had given to us. We decided that Stoney Creek should have a Homemakers Club.

At our first meeting several women came: Sophie Thomas, Mary Thomas, my sister-in-law Celena, and others. Mrs. Murphy helped us to apply for funding from the Indian Agent; we were given enough money to buy material for quilt-making and a sewing machine. I was made President of the Stoney Creek Homemakers.

In those early years, we were not political. We called ourselves the Busy Beavers and we were just what the name of our club said—we were busy homemakers, looking for ways to make life better for our families and our village. All of us were having babies and raising small children and we believed that we didn't have time for politics. We were still content to let the Indian Agent and the priest and the chief do our talking for us.

All this changed in 1976! We discovered in that year that we could no longer knit and crochet and quilt and leave Native politics to others.

July 1st, 1976. That holiday weekend, the Village of Vanderhoof was commemorating its fiftieth anniversary—in 1926 it had been incorporated as a village. The celebration, which went on during the long weekend, included a rodeo, a canoe race, a pancake breakfast, street dances, and an old-timers' reunion. Stoney Creek was almost empty, as the villagers flocked into town to eat and dance and take part in the festivities.

Early in the morning of July 3rd, just as dawn was breaking, the church bell in Stoney Creek began to toll. Only then did we know that death had visited our village again.

The news spread through Stoney Creek like wildfire—after the street dance ended in the early morning hours, Coreen Thomas, twenty-one years old and in her ninth month of pregnancy, had been struck by a car and killed as she walked back to Stoney Creek from Vanderhoof.

I stood with other villagers. We talked together in mournful little groups. Everyone had loved Coreen.

"Who brought the news?" asked one.

"Marjie—you know, her fifteen-year-old sister. She was there when the car hit Coreen."

"Poor little Marjie," said another. "She's crying and in a terrible state."

"They say Coreen's dad, Peter, wouldn't believe the Mountie when he said that Coreen had been killed. Peter has been taken to the morgue in the hospital so that he can see Coreen for himself."

"And the baby?"

"Dead too."

Oh, I thought, how terrible! Both mother and baby gone.

"Who was driving the car that hit Coreen?" someone asked.

"Richard Redekop."

"Not another Redekop!" said another. "Is that the brother of Stanley Redekop, the one with the pickup truck who hit Coreen's cousin, Larry Thomas, two years ago? The same family?"

"Yes, the same family."

I remembered the death of Larry Thomas, and the inquest that had followed it. The people of Stoney Creek were still bitter about the way in which that inquest had been conducted. Eric Turner was the coroner who had been in charge of the investigation into the death of Larry Thomas. It was said that the lawyer for the Thomas family was not notified about the hearing until one hour before it started, although he had to drive sixty miles from Prince George to Vanderhoof to attend. What upset us even more was that Larry's mother was picked up by an R.C.M.P. officer and put in jail just before the hearing into Larry's death started. The Mounties said that her talk was too loud. They let her go only when the inquest was over.

The people of Stoney Creek had never accepted the verdict of that inquest, which said that the driver of the pickup truck, Stanley Redekop, was not considered to have been responsible for Larry Thomas' death. We knew that there had been six people in the cab of the truck (where no more than two or three should have been) when it struck and killed Larry Thomas in 1974.

No, we had had bad feelings about that inquest at the time.

And now, another Thomas—really two, because Coreen was due to deliver her baby any day—had been struck and killed by another Redekop vehicle!

At the time of Coreen's death, Sophie Thomas was District Vice President of the Homemakers. She was also the aunt of Coreen and Larry Thomas. Sophie and I had been friends since we were children together. Like me, her marriage had been arranged; she was even younger than me, only fourteen, when she became a married woman. She had been active in the Homemakers from the beginning, and was more political, more of a speaker, than some of us. She was usually our delegate at the conferences in Vancouver or Duck Lake.

Sophie was heartsick when she learned of Coreen's death. She talked of the care Coreen had taken of her young brothers and sisters, the long lines of washing Coreen would hang out on the clothes line every week . . . and how she was looking forward to the birth of her baby! Sophie thought about having to go to the hospital and prepare Coreen and her baby for burial and she felt as if her heart was broken.

What could anyone say? Everyone shared in Sophie's grief.

One day soon after Coreen and her baby were killed, the Mounties sent word out to the village that they wanted to question Coreen's sister Marjie and another girl, Donna Patrick, about the accident. My daughter Helen accompanied Sophie Thomas and me to the police station in Vanderhoof with the girls.

I think my bad feelings about the R.C.M.P. and the coroner and the way in which they were handling Coreen's death began that afternoon. The two young girls were frightened and upset. They were taken into a room for questioning. Our request that one of us go in with them was refused. Instead, Sophie, Helen, and I sat on the steps of the police station for three hours, while the girls were being questioned inside the building. We were not even offered chairs to make our long wait more bearable.

When we read an account of Coreen's death in the Prince George paper, the *Citizen*, we became even more upset. The report said that Coreen had darted in front of the car which killed her. This did not agree with what Marjie Thomas, Donna Patrick, and others, had told us. They said that the driver of the car, Richard Redekop, had been driving too fast and that Coreen had no chance to get out of the vehicle's way. Some of the witnesses thought that the driver had aimed the car directly at Coreen—to them it looked as if he was playing the game, 'Get an Indian!'

Sophie talked to some of the village Homemakers. "I think," she said, "that bad things are happening to our people. I think we need help. I am going to phone Rose Charlie—she's president of the Homemakers in Vancouver. She will tell us what to do."

Within a very few days Kitty Bell, a member of the Vancouver Homemakers and active in publishing the paper *Indian Voice,* was in our area. From that moment, as Kitty began interviewing and investigating, Stoney Creek seemed to become a household name across Canada.

When I think back now to 1976, I remember headlines in papers and news flashes on the radio and television. That seemed to dominate our lives. Day after day, there was one revelation after another.

The headlines accused the white population of Vanderhoof of harassment of the Natives of Stoney Creek, and of R.C.M.P. indifference when the Natives complained. The B.C. branch of the Human Rights Commission soon became involved and said publicly that they were giving these charges of harassment top priority. By the middle of August, Bishop Remi De Roo, Chairman of the Human Rights Commission, was saying publicly that if even one-half of the report of Native abuse by whites in Vanderhoof was true, it was a heartbreaking situation. He found the Vanderhoof scene, he said, "explosive with a potential for very deep violence."

Rumours were flying through the village—rumours that some of the young Native witnesses had been threatened by the Mounties, and that these same Mounties were determined to make Coreen responsible for her own death. Meanwhile, although the R.C.M.P. said that they had a file on the accident that was about four inches thick, there was no sign that coroner Eric Turner intended to conduct an inquest or a public investigation into Coreen's death.

Our Homemakers club met, and it was agreed that Sophie Thomas would write to the Vanderhoof coroner. She did. She wrote, "The Homemakers club and band members are asking for a public inquest. Please advise."

At the same time, Eric Turner was reported in the paper to have said that after studying the whole case, he had decided that no inquest was necessary. A day or two later, however, he met Sophie as she and a number of Native children were boarding a bus for Prince George—the children were going to give a display of Native dancing.

"Do you really want an inquest?" Eric Turner asked Sophie. She told him that nothing less than an inquest would clear the air.

Shortly after this meeting, Eric Turner announced that he had set September 22nd as a possible date for an inquest into Coreen's death. He denied that he had been influenced by sensational headlines, and he said that he thought a night sitting should be long enough to cover the evidence.

This statement worried us. A quick one-night sitting could not answer the questions that troubled us. Was Richard Redekop travelling too fast when his vehicle hit Coreen? Had he been drinking that night and if so, how much? Did the Mounties try to force the young witnesses to say that Coreen had been playing 'chicken' with Redekop's car? What efforts had been made to save Coreen's baby?

Oh, the questions we had went on and on. They could never be answered in a short one-night sitting! Imagine our relief when we learned that the B.C. Homemakers had decided to hire Harry Rankin, Vancouver alderman and well-known lawyer, to act for the Stoney Creek Homemakers at the inquest. Harry must have contacted the news media right away. He did not think, he said, that anyone, even the coroner, could set a time limit on the length of time an inquest would take. "There are important ramifications to this case," said Harry.

The headlines on September 8, 1976, hit our village like a bombshell: VANDERHOOF CORONER WITHDRAWS FROM THE INQUEST; TURNER WANTS OUT; VANDERHOOF CORONER RECALLS OWN CONVICTION TEN YEARS AGO. We shook our heads in wonder. Well! Well! Well! we kept saying to each other.

One reporter wrote, "Coroner Eric Turner, 50, confirmed

that he drove away after hitting and killing a man on a highway near Prince George and didn't report the accident until
the next morning. . . . Turner confirmed that he was con-
victed but said that he could not remember the exact charge.
He thought it was public mischief and that he was fined three
hundred dollars. He also said that he could not remember
exactly when the accident occurred, nor the victim's name,
but believed that it happened about ten years ago. . . . Describing his own accident, Turner said he was driving late on a
stormy night near Prince George when a drunken man staggered in front of the car. . . . He said he panicked and drove
home, then turned himself in in the morning. . . . 'I never
really believed that things like that happened—people panick-
ing, going into a state of shock. It really does happen.' . . .
Turner said he told the head of the R.C.M.P. detachment of the
accident when he was being interviewed before his appoint-
ment as coroner in 1972."

When Turner withdrew, it was announced that the inquest
into Coreen's death would be held on September 25, 1976, in
the Vanderhoof Secondary School and that the Supervisor of
Coroners for British Columbia, Glen McDonald, would pre-
side. Like everyone else in Stoney Creek, I breathed a sigh of
relief when I heard about the change in coroners. I hoped that
with Mr. McDonald presiding, Natives' concerns would get a
full hearing.

In the meantime, Sophie Thomas, quoted in the *Toronto
Globe and Mail* and in *Maclean's* magazine, expressed what
we all felt: "I'm getting madder every day. If Coreen was not
a Native girl this all would have been handled differently.
Coreen was nine months pregnant when she died. During the
autopsy they removed the baby and her relatives buried her
with her unborn boy in her arms. That really hurt the Indian
people. They really shed a tear when they saw that baby."

Between the time that Coreen was killed and the beginning of the inquest on September 25th, I found out what it was to become political. Sophie Thomas was our spokesperson, but many other people in the village found themselves suddenly involved as they had never been involved before. My daughter Helen—at that time she was working as a cousellor for Native students attending St. Joseph's School in Vanderhoof—and I were in the thick of things.

So much needed doing. After the funeral of Coreen and her baby, there were many meetings around my big kitchen table. We had to make sure that people were available for the reporters to interview, that the group of young people who were with Coreen on the night of her death were available as witnesses, that people like Kitty Bell and Harry Rankin and staff from the Human Rights Commission had all the local help and information that they needed.

It seemed to me that we never stopped in those weeks between July 3rd and September 25th. For the first time, people like Sophie Thomas and my daughter Helen and Archie Patrick, a Native teacher, had a chance to tell the world what living conditions were really like in our village: the fact that the tuberculosis rate on the reserve was twenty times the national average, that our people were unemployed, that housing was deplorable with sometimes twelve and sixteen people living in two-room shacks, that the village needed sewers, and that despite our love of our village, we knew that it was one of the poorest and most backward reserves in central British columbia.

The eyes of the nation were on our village. Here was our chance to talk, and talk we did, about the poverty of our reserve, the lack of opportunity for our people, the racism that we had to deal with day after day, the stranglehold that the Department of Indian Affairs had over our lives.

I left most of the talking to others. I'm not a fighter or a talker—just like when I was a student in Lejac so many years ago, I'm timid and shy. But even so, there in the background, I was active. I wanted to make the Homemakers strong and I wanted, as much as Sophie or Archie or Harry Rankin or any of them, to see justice done to my people for once in my life.

Yes, those weeks in the summer of 1976 were weeks when we were really fired up. When they were over, those of us who were involved would never again be quite so satisfied to let others do the talking for us while we knitted and made our quilts and raised our families.

CHAPTER EIGHTEEN

WHAT FEELINGS WE ALL HAD AS THE day of the inquest, Saturday, September 25th, 1976, approached! Mixed with the excitement, we felt a sadness that the events of July 3rd would have to be relived. We worried about the shy and frightened young girls who would have to give evidence. We wanted to make sure that people like Harry Rankin would be comfortable staying on the reserve. Harry and his son-in-law, David, had sleeping quarters in my daughter Helen's home; most of their meals were taken at the kitchen table in my home.

September 25th was one of those fall days in central British Columbia that I loved even as a little girl—the sun had burned off the early morning fog by the time we arrived in the gymnasium of the secondary school in Vanderhoof, and we knew that the day was going to be as warm as a day in July.

Quite a sight met our eyes. Along one long table were reporters and journalists from across Canada. In the front of the gymnasium there was a table for the coroner, and to one side the jury was seated at another table—four Natives and two whites. The R.C.M.P. seemed to be everywhere, and I could see that there were a number of lawyers seated beside Harry Rankin—the Redekop and Thomas families each had a lawyer, and there was a lawyer from the Attorney General's Department. In the audience, my daughter Helen and I and our friends pointed out to each other various politicians, representatives from the Native Court-workers, the United Native Nations, the Human Rights Commission, the Department of Indian Affairs. I noticed that the ladies of Vanderhoof had set up a snack bar outside the gymnasium door and sold lots of soft drinks, coffee, and sandwiches.

When we arrived there were about fifty people in the audience, but all through the days and into the night sittings, people—white and Native—drifted in and out, so that the school gymnasium and the Legion Hall which had to be used for the last two days of the inquest, were often crowded.

Saturday, Sunday, Monday, Tuesday—the inquest went on and on. Except for the time that I spent with young witnesses such as Marjie Thomas and Donna Patrick, I never missed a minute of the proceedings.

Apart from the Mounties and some of the white people called by the lawyer for the Redekop family, I knew most of the witnesses well. It made me sad to hear those witnesses tell of the Native young people and the white young people calling out insults to each other as they walked up the hill going out of Vanderhoof in the early morning hours when the accident happened. And how hard it was to listen to the minute-by-minute details when the Redekop vehicle struck Coreen and sent her body flying across the road, the noise and confusion, the delay in getting help—oh, it was hard to listen to that!

It was hard to listen to the ambulance driver telling of taking Coreen's body into the morgue in the hospital without a doctor first certifying that she was dead, or without any medical attempt to save the baby's life. It was hard to listen to Coreen's sister Marjie tell of her interview with the Mountie. It hurt to hear her say, "The policeman was mean to me. He made me cry. I was scared," and to remember Helen and Sophie and me sitting on the steps of the police station, having been refused permission to go with the young girl when she was interviewed.

And what could I think when Marjorie and Donna Patrick said that the Mountie made them say that Coreen was playing 'chicken' and that she was darting out at vehicles and jumping back at the last minute? The girls said that the Mountie forced them to make such a statement, and then accused them of lying when they said this statement wasn't true.

So much of the evidence was confusing to me, and, I think, to most of the people listening—the evidence about skid marks and the speed of vehicles and blood tests for alcohol and the oxidation of alcohol in the blood—these things meant more to the lawyers and the coroner than they did to me.

We did learn in those hours and hours of testimony that Richard Redekop was probably travelling at least thirty-seven to forty miles an hour in a thirty-mile zone when his vehicle struck Coreen, that he had a blood alcohol count of .08 one hour after the accident, and that Coreen may have been re-fused admission to the room in the Vanderhoof Hotel which she had rented for the night, forcing her to walk back to Stoney Creek. And through much of the proceedings, especially when the R.C.M.P. or other professionals were testifying, I had the feeling that what Sophie Thomas had said earlier was right—that if Coreen had not been a Native girl, every-thing would have been handled differently.

———————

My daughter Helen and I had heard that reporters from the CBC, *Maclean's* magazine, *The Globe and Mail*, and many other representatives of the news media wanted to interview several people. We thought that a meal would be a good way to get people together. On Monday night, September 27th, my family invited reporters and any other interested persons out to the reserve for dinner, served on my big kitchen table. We had salads, fried chicken, bannock, pies—you name it, we served it! But better than all the food was to see white and Native people sitting in my kitchen and living room, talking together. Many of the journalists and reporters, some of them from as far away as Toronto and Montreal, had never been on a reservation before, or eaten a meal with a Native in a Native's home.

The chief was there, Harry Rankin, Archie Patrick, Sophie Thomas, most of the Homemakers—they were all interviewed, and then the talk really began! It was a night to remember.

Finally, on Tuesday, September 28th, after Mayor McLeod, Richard Redekop, and Eric Turner had taken the stand, the jury retired to consider the evidence.

When the foreman, Chief Ken Luggi of the Stellaquo Band, stood up to read the jury's verdict, you could hear a pin drop in the packed Legion Hall. Close to the front sat Coreen's mother and father and their daughter Marjie.

"We find," read Ken Luggi, "that Richard Redekop was negligent, in that the vehicle he was driving was moving too fast through a crowd of people on a relatively narrow road during hours of darkness."

The jury made several recommendations: that police and ambulance and other emergency services in Vanderhoof be up-graded; that people not be placed in a morgue until a death certificate was issued; that in accident cases, breathalyzer tests be taken as quickly as possible; that the R.C.M.P. be encouraged to have a parent or guardian present when witnesses sixteen years old or younger were questioned; that the

Stoney Creek Band and Vanderhoof Council work together to establish a Friendship Centre.

The Prince George paper, the *Citizen,* reported afterwards that Natives hugged each other and cried as they realized that their concerns in this case had also been the jury's. The paper also showed a picture of Richard Redekop and his lawyer studying a written report of the jury's verdict.

Like many other people in Stoney Creek, I slept better that night in the belief that justice had, for once, been done.

Helen and I, Sophie Thomas and our Homemakers Club attended many meetings and sat on many committees to set up a Friendship Centre where whites and Natives could come to know each other better. Nothing came of these meetings. No Friendship Centre was built, but maybe the two communities understood each other a little better because of the effort.

Meanwhile, the case of Richard Redekop dragged on. Coreen's parents laid a charge of criminal negligence against him—the prosecutor refused to proceed with the case because, said the prosecutor's office, there was insufficient evidence to proceed with the charge. Finally, as Coreen's parents and our Homemakers Club continued to press for charges against Redekop, the Attorney General's Department intervened and months later, Richard Redekop was finally charged. After two days of hearings, again in the Legion Hall in Vanderhoof, the judge dismissed the charges. That dismissal came very soon after Donna Patrick admitted that she had been lying when she gave evidence that the R.C.M.P. had forced her to make statements that Coreen had been playing chicken.

I think we were all stunned when Richard Redekop walked out of court, all charges against him dropped. I remember that I sat there, unable to believe that all our efforts had ended in 'charges dismissed.' What an end to my first venture into politics!

CHAPTER NINETEEN

THINGS SEEMED TO GO FLAT AFTER Richard Redekop's trial. There were meetings with Vanderhoof residents and with groups like the Human Rights Commission about a Friendship House, where whites and Natives could get together. Nothing came of the hours my daughter Helen and I, Archie Patrick, Sophie Thomas, and many others spent talking about where such a place would be, how it should be run, where the funding would come from. In the end, like so many other good things, the idea was just talked to death.

For a couple of years, things jogged along as usual in Stoney Creek. We worked as we had always done, generation after generation. All the headlines of 1976 didn't seem to bring any changes to our village—we were still one of the poorest reserves in British Columbia. Our young people were still unemployed, our living conditions were still bad. The statements that Sophie Thomas and Archie Patrick and Kitty Bell had made to reporters in 1976 could have been made again, two years after Coreen Thomas' death.

Then in 1978, tragedy struck my family and within days, death came to other families on the reserve as well. On a hot summer day, July 6, 1978, my son Ernie phoned me from Prince George. His truck had broken down. He asked my daughter Helen and I to come to Prince George and pick him up. This was not as simple as it sounded; Helen's car was in a garage in Vanderhoof, having some repair work done. We stopped in at my son Charles' home to see if we could catch a ride into Vanderhoof to get Helen's car. At the time, Charles was thirty-six, married to Gracie. They had three children. Gracie drove us into Vanderhoof. We picked up Helen's car and went on our way. Unknown to us, that was the last time Helen and I would see Charles alive.

On our return to the village, there was a big commotion going on. Charles and some of his friends had gone swimming in Nulki Lake. The other swimmers had returned to the beach after their swim, but Charles had disappeared in the bay. Already, on our return from Prince George, a search party had been formed by some of the men in the village and the R.C.M.P.

For one night and one day, the search for his body went on. On the shore, my daughters and I set up a camp to serve food and coffee to the searchers. Before many hours passed, we found that we weren't the only camp on the shore. Three hundred yards down the beach from us, another fire was burning and here other villagers and friends were gathered, not to help, but to party. Hour after hour, as police and band members searched the bay, I saw drunk people staggering around, I heard their loud voices talking and singing.

To lose Charles, and not to know where his body was, was almost more than we could bear. But to watch that other party and to have to listen to them—oh, that was terrible!

Finally, Charles' body was found, but by then another tragedy had stunned our village. Just before Charles' body was taken from the lake, a twenty-year-old boy who had been drinking on the shore staggered up to the village. In his home, he took a gun and shot himself. Within days, another young lad shot himself, and shortly after that, a fourth boy over-dosed with drugs and died.

The village was in shock.

In less than four weeks, we had lost four of our young men, one by drowning, two with bullets and one through drugs. At first, stunned with grief, we could only shake our heads and say to each other, "What next?"

It was my daughter Helen and Archie Patrick from the Vanderhoof School District who decided to do something about the bad things which were happening in our vil-lage—they contacted other reserves and Victoria, and when that was done, it was decided that an Elders Society should be started in Stoney Creek.

When we started our Homemakers Club back in the for-ties, the purpose was to make us better wives and mothers. We learned crafts, we informed ourselves about child care and about anything else that would make our families healthier and happier. Little by little, as the years went by, we had fewer and fewer meetings of the Homemakers Club, until, by 1978, we hadn't had a meeting for nearly two years.

The Elders Society was different. For one thing, the Home-makers were all women, but our Elders Society has always had both men and women in it. And you don't have to be a certain age to belong to the Elders. There are about thirty of us who are active in the society. Some, like Lazare and I and my sister-in-law Celena, are getting old, but there are many of the members who are much younger than we are.

When we started, we thought that if we could revive our culture, maybe our young people would have more pride, and the bad things which had been happening, especially to our young men, might not happen any more. We started inviting people from other reserves in Alberta and the United States, to speak on aboriginal culture, and to talk about how drugs and alcohol had almost destroyed the Native people. These people from Alberta and the United States had gone through bad things in their own villages and they came to help us by telling us of their experiences.

One of the first things our Elders Society took on was the problem of school dropouts. We had so many young people in the village who had quit school and who were getting into trouble because they were hanging around the village with nothing to do. We started an alternate school in the basement of the kindergarten school on the reserve. We had the help of teachers from a religious group in Vanderhoof who sent people out to teach regular classes in the morning. In the afternoon elders like myself taught Indian crafts and Indian culture. We showed the young people how to treat hides, how to make snowshoes—oh, we taught them many things. The first year we had twelve students. Many of them returned to the regular school after a few months in our alternate classes.

Unfortunately for us, the teacher upstairs in the school complained that the hides had a bad smell which filled her room. We knew the school basement wasn't the right place for our alternate school, but what could we do? It was the only place we had.

It was at this time that we began to talk about a building which would belong to the Elders Society and in which we could do our own thing. Out of that talk came the Potlatch House which we have today.

The first step was to get land. Fortunately, the Elders had a good chief behind them, Gerald Casimer. He helped to pass a Band Council Resolution in 1980, giving our society the land, fifty acres in all. Twice we had to clear that land—we would clear it, but before we could get the money and logs to start building, the land needed clearing again!

Finally, we received $93,000 from the Agricultural Rural Development Agency (ARDA), which provides government funding for Native economic development. The Department of Manpower funded workers who began to put up the building. Members of the Elders Society cut and peeled the logs themselves, but even with this help, the building of our Potlatch House seemed to take forever!

The Potlatch House is up now; there is also a caretaker's house and an outside cookhouse where all the cooking and eating can be done. We had our first assembly in the Potlatch House in 1985. Since then, it has been used for weddings, potlatches, and gatherings of all kinds. The Elders hope before too long to have ten cabins and a recreational vehicle camp on the land along the shore of Nulki Lake. We want to make this project self-sufficient, to build it up so that in the future the young people can run it as a business. And when that is finished we want to start building an old Indian village on the other side of the road as a tourist attraction.

The Elders have great plans, all of them directed at building for the future. It is our hope that the young people will have a business to run and that this business will give them pride in their heritage and culture.

The Elders Society assists the Band Council whenever help is needed, and we support many activities in the village such as the Tigers, our village ball team.

We try to revive some of the traditional Native games as well. One that Lazare teaches is called the snow snake. This snow snake is a stick about seven feet long. It is narrow and it has a head like a snake. The stick is waxed until it is smooth and shiny. In the old days, each person had a snow snake—the snake was thrown, and whoever threw it the greatest distance won the game. This was a very popular traditional winter sport which Lazare taught the young people of our village.

Until two years ago, I was very active in what we called our survival camp. This camp was held in Wedgewood, the same spot where my parents fished and hunted and trapped so many years ago. It is passed down from generation to generation and in this way, has come to me.

The idea of the survival camp was to teach our young people how to survive if things got worse. We taught them that as long as they had a canoe and a net and a gun, they could go into the bush and survive. We taught them all kinds of ways to cook fish—boiling, barbecuing, smoking—and we showed them how to use the head and the backbone of the fish. We never wasted anything. We showed them how to cook bannock, to set a net, to can or dry fish, to strip and tan hides, to pick roots and make birch bark baskets, where to look for berries, how to bake bread in a cast iron pan buried in hot ashes. We would take only the necessities to the survival camp with us—for the rest, we depended on the river and the land around us to provide us with food.

The survival camp was very popular. I would invite anyone who wanted to come with me, and that too is an old tradition. Besides some of the elders and the young people from the village, we would have police officers, and many times other white people would join us. During one of the last years of the survival camp—we had to stop because of my health problems, my friend Veronica George was getting too old to handle it, and no one else turned up to take it over—we had four elders, five other adults from the village, and over twenty children. That year the survival camp went on for three weeks. We had the cabin that Lazare had built so long ago, and tents. I stayed in the cabin but everyone else wanted to stay in a tent. We had a cook shack, just poles and a roof, where there were tables and an old cook stove and a campfire that was kept going.

Of course, one of the problems we had with our camp at Wedgewood was vandalism. I had my canoe stolen one year, and another year, people who might have been from Prince George—we found penny matches with markings—wrecked our camp. They put a tree over the cabin and scattered our dishes all through the bush. The problem is that the cabin is up on the hill and it can be seen when people are going down the river.

Even so, until my health caused problems, we didn't let theft or vandalism get us down—we knew that we had so much to learn from each other that a stolen canoe or a tree over the cabin wasn't going to stop us from sharing our skills with anyone who wanted to learn them.

CHAPTER TWENTY

IF 1978 WAS A YEAR OF SADNESS for our village, it was also a year of new beginnings.

1979 was something else! The first big surprise came early in the year: the Rotary Club in Vanderhoof named me Citizen of the Year! As far as I know, a Native had never been nominated for this honour before.

This is what happened: one day in January, 1979, Eileen Kimball sent word for me to meet her at her home in Vanderhoof. She was a white woman, a teacher of handicapped children in Vanderhoof and a close friend of my daughter Helen. I didn't want to leave the reserve—I was very busy at the time, sewing and making things to get some money together. Our family was getting ready to put on a potlatch to make a pay-out for my son Charles' funeral.

The message from Eileen said, "Just come as you are," and that's exactly what I did. I didn't clean up or change my clothes or anything. Helen's husband, Don, drove me to Eileen's home in Vanderhoof, where I thought she and I were going to have a meeting of some kind. Of course everyone else, including Helen and Don, knew what was in store for me.

When I arrived at Eileen Kimball's home, she said, "We have to go to the Village Inn. The meeting is there."

I said, "I can't go there dressed like this!"

She and Don said, "Never mind! You look just fine!" and hustled me out the door.

Well! We walked into the Village Inn, and I could see that we were in the Banquet Room and that the long table was set for a big lunch. And then the news was broken to me—I was the guest of honour that day!

I could have crawled through the floor. I had no idea of anything, no speech, nothing!

Afterwards the local paper reported:

Mary John, a Stoney Creek resident, has won the Vanderhoof Rotary Club's 1978 award as Citizen of the year. Rotary Club president, Don McFetridge, made the announcement in front of 50 people at the year end Rotary luncheon.

The most surprised person in the room was Mary John, who was taken to the meeting by an associate, Eileen Kimball, who told her they were there to attend a meeting. Mary John told the gathering, 'I thought I was going to get a cheque to help the defunct drop-in centre reopen.'

Obviously pleased with her award, Mrs. John was originally educated on the Nahzli reserve before a school was built at Lejac, B.C., which she attended until Grade Eight.

'Her contributions to the communities of this area are of courageous undertaking as she set out to revive the nearly lost language and art of the Carrier,' said McFetridge.

Mrs. John was recognized for three areas in which local people hold her in high regard. The first is the family, where three of her eight children have created businesses of their own, the second is Stoney Creek and other Indian Communities, where she has worked hard counselling others and taking steps to maintain Carrier culture, and the third area is working in the white community in Vanderhoof in various jobs and community service organizations. Included are jobs with St. John Hospital and St. Joseph's School. The award is presented annually by the Rotary Club.

All I could do was thank the citizens of Vanderhoof for this honour, and tell them that it was a great surprise to me.

When I had time to think about it afterwards, I thought how times had changed! At the time of Coreen Thomas' death, someone had described my village and Vanderhoof as Two Solitudes, close together as the crow flies, but far apart in every other way. When I read that, I thought, "How true!" The people of the two communities could not have been more divided if a wide ocean had separated them. When I was a child, and even when I was a grown woman, there were so many businesses in Vanderhoof that my people and I could not enter. And now I was an honoured citizen, recognized by many of the same business people in that same town. Strange!

———————

In the middle of that year, 1979, there was another surprise for me and my husband Lazare.

On June 11th, 1979, we had been married for fifty years. If I could have had my wish on that day, I would have had Lazare and me repeat our marriage vows, but since that wasn't possible, we made do with Mass in our village church. Before I went to Mass, I saw a beautiful new Ford pickup truck with a canopy parked near by. "Gee," I said, "I wish that truck was mine!"

Imagine the surprise Lazare and I felt, when we returned from Mass, to find more than one hundred people—family and friends—at our home. And there was that same truck decorated with streamers and a big 50 sign, a gift to us from our family.

What a day that was! It was a perfect June afternoon; the sun was shining, and there were family members and friends and tables of food wherever I looked in the yard. When I had time to get over the shock I wrote the following letter to my family and friends, published in the local paper:

> I want to thank you all for Lazare and myself, for joining us on our 50th anniversary. Also for the many gifts you have so generously given us.

But, most of all, I want to thank you for your friendship to us over the years. Your kindness and encouragement has gotten us this far. We couldn't have done it without friends. So God bless you all. A special thank you to my family for our new vehicle and for their love and consideration. I wouldn't trade any of you for all the millions in the world. I'd like to close with a few lines from a poem I read: 'Grow old along with me, the best is yet to be, the last from which the first was made. Trust God, see all, don't be afraid.' God bless you, Mary John Senior.

Late that evening, when all the guests had departed and it was so quiet that I could hear the frogs in Stoney Creek, I thought back to fifty years ago. I remembered the little sixteen-year-old girl and the twenty-one-year-old boy, each so shy, who knew nothing of each other. I remembered the teasing aunt who shouted at me as I crouched in the corner of my family's cabin, "Why are you crying? Tonight, you are going to sleep with your husband!" I remembered Lazare coming into the cabin and saying to me, "Come." And I remembered that walk from the Paul cabin to the John cabin and my stern mother-in-law. Only five minutes was needed to cover the distance, no more, but it seemed to me to be the longest walk in my life.

Who would have thought then that fifty years later, this couple would still be alive and together?

Around about the time that I was named Citizen of the Year, Lazare and I started thinking about building another house, this time on the shore of Nulki Lake, but still on reserve land.

Years before, one of my heroes, Bill Grant, was our Indian Agent. I think that every paper in Canada described how he lost his job and almost ended up in jail because he had helped Native people in the north to get better housing with plumbing and sewage. In 1958 while he was still Indian Agent in Vanderhoof, before he had this trouble, he had offered to build Lazare and me a house on reserve land much closer to Vanderhoof. At the time, I was working in the hospital. It would have made life easier for me, but I didn't want to leave the house in Stoney Creek that Lazare and I had worked so hard to build. Also, I wanted to be in our own village when the kids were growing up. I wanted to be part of everything.

Twenty years later, things had changed. Our children were all grown up and on their own and the house that was almost new in 1958 was beginning to show signs of wear and tear. Besides, we had a big herd of cattle, and people were complaining about our livestock roaming around the village. Our daughter Florence and her husband George had a growing family and a very small house. Lazare and I thought that we would build a new house for ourselves, and this daughter of ours and her family could live in our old house.

I knew exactly what I wanted in this new home. First of all, I wanted a warm place for Lazare and me to enjoy in our old age. I wanted a basement with a furnace, so that the floors would be warm. I wanted a big kitchen, a big living room and a big bedroom—no little teeny rooms for me!

How we worked! It took us all summer to get the logs ready. Then the Department of Indian Affairs was slow coming through with the money ($10,000) to which we were entitled, and that meant that what we should have completed in the fall wasn't started until winter. We worked all through the winter. How hard that was! Plenty of times the floors inside were so thick with ice that we could hardly move inside the building.

All my life I had wanted a nice log house, located where I could look out and see the lake. I wanted to see the sun rise and set from the shore of the lake, I wanted to see the storms as they moved across the water, and I wanted to see and hear the return of the geese to the marsh in the spring. I guess when you have been brought up in poverty, and you are raising a family in poverty, there is nothing you want so much as a nice home. For me, the home of my dreams was always a log house on Nulki Lake.

Although after much hard work and hardship I had the house I had always wanted, not everything worked out as we had planned. Not long after we moved to our new home, we had to sell our herd of cattle in order to pay for a lawyer for our son Ernie. We were very emotional about that, not with Ernie, but with the Department of Indian Affairs and the way in which that department used our son.

Ernie had started a logging business and it seemed to me and my family that right from the start, the Department of Indian Affairs was out to break him. I don't know—sometimes I think the Department people don't want the Native people to make anything of themselves. We heard reports that the District Manager of the Department was holding secret meetings with other people from our village, and the next thing we knew, when acres of logs had been cut and Ernie was making quite a bit of money for the Band, the Department of Indian Affairs took the logging contract away from him. Lazare and I tried to assist Ernie in his struggle with the Department, and that is why we had to sell our cattle. The money from the sale didn't help. Ernie lost his logging business in spite of the money we spent.

All those logs—people came from all directions, sawed them up for firewood and drove off with their loads. These were logs that could have meant homes or money in the bank for our village people. Instead, they just went up in flames.

CHAPTER TWENTY-ONE

NOWADAYS, MANY WHITE PEOPLE COME to my home, but years ago this was not the case. For many years the only white person to come into my kitchen was the priest. I used to prepare breakfast for him after Mass. I felt so proud to have someone white eating at my table. I thought that was a real treat for me.

One other non-Native used to drop in regularly, and that was the writer, Rich Hobson, who wrote *Grass Beyond the Mountain, Nothing's Too Good for a Cowboy*, and many other best sellers. He used to pass our place on his way into town from his ranch. He had a Native boy, a cousin of mine, who drove his vehicle for him. Rich would wash up at my house, I'd make him a cup of coffee, and then he'd be on his way into Vanderhoof. What a good and friendly man he was!

But for many years, except for Rich Hobson and the priest, we were a race apart. Even now, we sometimes feel like that. We begin to hope that racism is a thing of the past, and then we have an experience which shows us that not much has changed.

The worst experience I had with racism in recent years was

when I became sick in 1984. A young friend of mine, Judy, took me to Outpatients in the hospital where I had worked for so many years—I was miserable, short of breath, and with bad chest pains. A new doctor, a surgeon, gave me a brief examination. When he was finished, a nurse I knew came to me and said, "Did you have any lunch, Mary?"

"I had a late breakfast," I answered.

This new doctor was standing nearby and he said, "Oh, just give her lots of moosemeat!"

I thought that was really something, coming from a doctor. A true racial slur! It bothered me, but I was too sick to say anything. I was admitted with congestive heart failure and was a patient for quite a while. Finally, I was discharged.

Before long, I had a relapse, and when I was admitted to the hospital again, the same doctor appeared on the ward. He stopped by my bed."

You must like this hotel," he said. "Nice hotel, eh?"

I was angry. "I'm not here because I like it. I'm here because I'm sick!"

I complained to the head nurse and to two doctors I knew, Doctor Mooney and Doctor Jolly. "I think it's rude the way that doctor talks to patients from the reserve," I said. "You can't talk to people like that, especially when they're as sick as I am! I already feel sorry for myself and he makes it worse!"

Someone must have talked to him. The next time he came around, he said nothing. He just patted me on the back.

———————

This sickness in 1984 stopped me from taking part in the survival camp and setting nets when the fish were running, but once I was out of the hospital for the second time and rested up, I found myself busier than ever with other things.

We have a Welfare Committee in our village which plans for Native children when families have a problem. Many of the meetings of this committee are held in my home. We call the parents to a conference and talk to them about their troubles, whether their problems are financial or drinking or whatever. If it is better for the children to be apart from the parents until the problems are solved, we try to find a home for the little ones in our village; if this is not possible, we scrounge on other reserves for a foster home. Over the years, many Stoney Creek children have been placed in non-Native foster and adoption homes, often far away from Stoney Creek, and have lost their heritage forever. We want to make sure that this can never happen again to a child from our village.

When our son Charles drowned, we learned that the R.C.M.P. were not just there to throw a person in jail—we learned that they were there to help, too. The officer who looked for Charles' body was just like one of us. Because we remember the help we had then, every year since that bad time, my family and I put on a dinner—bannock, smoked fish, and all the trimmings, for the Vanderhoof detachment of the R.C.M.P. And if we are ever late in having this get-together for one reason or another, the officers always manage to remind us that we have a date with them!

The biggest project I have now is the potlatch place and with it, the teaching of our young people about our culture. The elders and I teach many things—scraping and treating hides, beadwork, spinning wool, making baskets, drying and canning fish. They come to me, these young people, and say, "Mary, can you help me with this hide?" or "Mary, I waste a lot of this fish I'm dryingwhen I cut out the big bone in the back. Show me what I'm doing wrong." I smile when I hear the young voices asking for help or instruction—they sound like me fifty years ago or more, when I would come to Bella or my mother with a hide or a piece of bead-work that I could not manage!

Lazare, now in his eighties, is like me—always on the go! He was very sick with pneumonia in the winter of 1985, and more recently, he had a cataract operation and a cornea transplant. The doctor told him after the transplant, "Stay very quiet; don't bend down or exert yourself in any way." The doctor light as well have saved his breath! Lazare paid no more attention to him than he does to the rain or the cold. He's forever cleaning up the yard, raking leaves in the summer and shovelling snow in the winter. He can't see to hunt or trap any more, but he still goes out into the bush with the boys, passing on to them the wisdom he has learned over the years. At those times, he tramps through the bush with the best of them and does his share in making camp with them overnight.

And perhaps, best of all, with seven children still living, with thirty-two grandchildren and eighteen great-grandchildren, most of them living close by, our log house near the lake is never lonely.

EPILOGUE

OFTEN WHEN I GO TO BED AT NIGHT I think about all the people who lived in our village and are now gone—my daughter Helen, my son Charles, my half-brother Mark, my stepsister Bella, my mother and Johnny Paul, Lazare's mother and father, and many, many others—all gone from us.

And sometimes, as I remember them, I wonder what they would think if they could see Stoney Creek now.

The creek itself is the same, maybe a little lazier than it used to be, and the hillocks that I loved as a child are still there. But the log cabins are gone, and every year, a few more old houses disappear, to be replaced by modern bungalows, brightly painted and as modern as any home in the city.

I'll bet that my mother and Johnny Paul would be surprised at all the labour-saving devices on the reserve today. In the old days, everyone worked so hard. There were no tools, often nothing more than an axe, a sharp knife and bare hands. Many people in the white community had it hard too, but on the reserves, everybody, every single person, had it hard. Now we have power tools of all kinds. Imagine! I have a little tractor that I sit on and cut the grass right down to the edge of the lake! In the night I wonder what my mother and Johnny would think of that and I smile to myself in the dark.

And I remember our trips to Vanderhoof with a wagon and horses and Johnny holding the reins, pulling the horses up tight when we descended the hill into Vanderhoof. What would he think now if he could see the number of cars and trucks in the village? Wouldn't he and my mother be surprised if they saw me or one of my children get into a car and drive to Vancouver or Edmonton with less fuss than we used to have going to Vanderhoof or Lejac? Maybe the speed we have now is better, but many times I think that I'd give anything for just one more trip behind the horses in Johnny Paul's wagon!

In the night I think of the pension cheques Lazare and I get every month, and I remember that when our forefathers reached our age, there was no government help for them—the Band or their families looked after them. Later, when the old age pension started, I remember my mother-in-law, Lazare's mother, getting a pension cheque for eight dollars. How happy she was! Now our children don't have to worry about us. We get our cheques, we do what we want to do, and still the money comes in every month. We look forward to that, to being able to pay our bills. That is one change we really like.

And there are some things that I know Lazare's parents and my parents would not like—the drugs, the alcohol, the young people who will not listen to their elders. They would miss the closeness that there used to be in our village. Years ago we spent a lot of time visiting one another, drinking tea at homemade tables in each other's cabin. There isn't much of that anymore. Now, everyone seems to be busy doing their own thing, and when they are finished, they sit at home and watch television. I sigh when I remember how many years it is since a house was cleared of its furniture, the fiddles were tuned up and we danced the night away!

Someone asked me once, "If you had three wishes for your people, what would they be?"

I have often thought about that question. My answer is always the same—I would wish for better living conditions on the reserves, more education for our young people, and a chance for them to find employment on the reservations. Yes, my three wishes never change.

Gradually, living conditions in my own village are getting better. Many of the things that we talked about as late as 1976 when Coreen Thomas was killed have improved—we now have plumbing and sewage, and people are not crowded ten and twelve into a shack the way that they were even ten years ago. Every year, a few new homes go up in the village. So living conditions in Stoney Creek have improved, but sometimes I feel as if the improvements are coming too slowly. And I know that while a few houses may be going up in our village each year, there are other reserves where living conditions are still terrible. Lots of young couples in our province and in Canada are forced to give up reserve life be cause there isn't decent housing. They want something better for their children than they had when they were growing up.

Often when I think about education and employment for our young people, I feel bitter. It seems that young people have to get off the reserve in order to get an education or to find a job. They cannot get either if they stay on the reservations. We are kind of fenced in. It is very hard to get anywhere on the reserve, or so it seems to have been in my lifetime. In my own case, when I was working, I had to move to town in order to be sure that I could get to work.

What upsets me most is that on the reserve, so many young people have nothing to live for. People like Lazare and me, we do our daily round of chores as we have always done, but we no longer have to think about making a living. With our young people it is different. I know that when they have no employment, they have no reason to get up in the morning. As I get older it worries me that the young people, without jobs, without hope, have no future in our Native villages.

I feel as if the reserves are both a kind of a trap and a protection for us. More and more I see our young people moving to the city, and who can blame them for that? But when they leave their villages, many of them lose contact with their own people and the old way of life.

Our culture is very important to us. I believe that if we lose our language, our dances, our music, our tales handed down from generation to generation by our elders, we lose what is our country to us. It is good to live well like white people, but we must hang on to what was ours and what was good in the old ways.

We must keep our language, our culture, and our land so that, even in Canada, we can still feel that we have our own country. And while we preserve these things, it is my hope that some day we will also have reserves where the young can be educated, where there is employment for all and where my people will choose to live, and work, and finally, to die and rest in peace.

BRIDGET MORAN was born in Northern Ireland in 1923, and came to Success, Saskatchewan with her family as a child. She served in the Women's Royal Canadian Naval Service between 1944 and 1946, graduated from the University of Toronto in 1950, and in 1951, after one year's graduate studies, went to British Columbia to work as a social worker for the provincial social welfare department. She was suspended by W.AC. Bennett's government in 1964 for public criticisms of welfare servces, especially as they related to children. Although she won reinstatement, she was told there would be no job for her nor did it appear that there ever would be.

From 1977 to 1989, she was a social worker with the Prince George School District. In addition, she worked as a freelance journalist, her work appearing frequently on CBC and in the *Vancouver Sun.* She retired in 1989, but not before starting her new career as a writer with the publication of *Stoney Creek Woman* in 1988. She went on to write three other books also published by Arsenal Pulp Press: *Judgement at Stoney Creek* (1990), the account of the inquest into the hit-and-run death of a young pregnant Carrier Native, Coreen Thomas; *A Little Rebellion* (1992), Bridget's own story about her experiences as a provincial social worker; and *Justa: A First Nations Leader* (1994), the biography of Carrier tribal chief Justa Monk. She is also the author of *Prince George Remembered,* a chapbook she self-published in 1996.

In 1992, Bridget and Mary John received the Governor General's Medal commemorating Canada's 125th anniversary as a confederation. In 1995, Bridget was awarded an honorary law degree from the University of Northern British Columbia in Prince George, and in 1996 received another honorary law degree from the University of Victoria. She served on the boards of the College of New Caledonia in Prince George, and the Legal Services Society of B.C. In addition, she is the mother of two sons and two daughters, and is also a grandmother.

Bridget passed away in 1999.